I0213536

ENDORSEMENTS

Do you ever wonder where God is in the midst of your pain? Do you sometimes question whether God really loves you and is concerned about your situation? If some of this describes you, then you are not alone! Dr. Joe and Heidi Wadlinger describe the emotions and frustrations they experienced while waiting for the healing in Joe's body to manifest.

One of the keys they discovered is that healing is not merely an event! Often, healing can be a journey. You will love the way Joe and Heidi describe the difficult and yet glorious way the Lord led them into their journey for healing. Their book *Healed!* is like sitting in a living room and having a conversation with them.

I recommend *Healed!* to anyone needing healing or anyone who desires to be used by God for helping others to receive healing. This book will change your life and your walk with the Lord!

BARBARA WENTROBLE
www.barbarawentroble.com
Founder, International Breakthrough Ministries;
Breakthrough Business Network
Author of nine books including: *Fighting for Your Prophetic Promises, Empowered for Your Purpose, Prophetic Intercession,* and *Praying With Authority*

This book is an inspiring true story of one couple's journey from sickness to wholeness. When we first met Dr. Joe and Heidi, Joe was essentially immobile and writhing in pain from a nerve condition in his body. This condition had resulted in him giving up his career and basically being homebound. They began attending our church and immediately grabbed hold of the Word of God that promises healing to those who will believe.

It was a process, but day by day we saw improvement. I can remember the pain Joe suffered while waiting for the total manifestation of his healing, but he would not give up on the promise of God. Anytime there was an opportunity, he was there and always the first to respond to the call for prayer. Joe and Heidi spoke the promises of God, not what they saw. Even when his healing was 90 percent and then 95 percent, he would not settle for anything less than a total 100 percent manifested healing.

This book is a must read for anyone who is struggling with a health issue. It will build your faith as you see how God remembers His covenant between Himself and His creation. You will see the power of confessing the Word of God over your situation to bring about God's promised end. And you will see the love of God in the process.

DONNA WISE
Senior Pastor: Impact Church International
President, Genesis...A New Beginning
www.impactci.org

No matter where an individual is in his or her faith walk; no matter what they believe about God and His power to save, heal, and redeem; no matter how distorted a person's theology may be; a personal testimony has the ability to bring hope, even to our hardest trials and deepest pain.

Dr. Joe and Heidi Wadlinger remind us of how important and how life changing a personal testimony can be to the most hopeless situations. *Healed!* is a book filled with hope that proclaims to us all, "You too can be healed." It reminds us that Jesus really is the Healer and that it is the testimony of our healing that reveals the nature and character of the God we serve.

Thank you, Joe and Heidi, for never giving up, never compromising what you believe, never listening to the naysayers. Thank you for fighting the good fight and teaching us all to not give in or to settle for the plans of the enemy! Thank you for reminding us who we are in Christ! Thank you for reminding us that we too have a powerful testimony of the healing power of Jesus.

And as we tell others, we can join you in spreading hope to our generation in desperate need of the hope only found in Him!

ALEX BAREFOOT
Lead Pastor, Eastside Community Church
www.eastsidechurch.co

HEALED!

HEALED!

GOD'S BREAKTHROUGH BLUEPRINT FOR
RECEIVING AND RELEASING MIRACLES

DR. JOE & HEIDI WADLINGER

© Copyright 2019– Dr. Joe and Heidi Wadlinger

All rights reserved. This book is protected by the copyright laws of the United States of America. This book may not be copied or reprinted for commercial gain or profit. The use of short quotations or occasional page copying for personal or group study is permitted and encouraged. Permission will be granted upon request. Unless otherwise identified, Scripture quotations are taken from the New King James Version. Copyright © 1982 by Thomas Nelson, Inc. Used by permission. All rights reserved. Scripture quotations marked NIV are taken from the HOLY BIBLE, NEW INTERNATIONAL VERSION®, Copyright © 1973, 1978, 1984, 2011 International Bible Society. Used by permission of Zondervan. All rights reserved. Scripture quotations marked NLT are taken from the Holy Bible, New Living Translation, copyright 1996, 2004, 2015. Used by permission of Tyndale House Publishers, Wheaton, Illinois 60189. All rights reserved. Scripture quotations marked TLB are taken from The Living Bible; Tyndale House, 1997, © 1971 by Tyndale House Publishers, Inc. Used by permission. All rights reserved. Scripture quotations marked KJV are taken from the King James Version. All emphasis within Scripture quotations is the author's own. Please note that Destiny Image's publishing style capitalizes certain pronouns in Scripture that refer to the Father, Son, and Holy Spirit, and may differ from some publishers' styles. Take note that the name satan and related names are not capitalized. We choose not to acknowledge him, even to the point of violating grammatical rules.

DESTINY IMAGE® PUBLISHERS, INC.

P.O. Box 310, Shippensburg, PA 17257-0310

"Promoting Inspired Lives."

This book and all other Destiny Image and Destiny Image Fiction books are available at Christian bookstores and distributors worldwide.

Cover design by Joseph J. Wadlinger, III and Eileen Rockwell
Interior design by Terry Clifton

For more information on foreign distributors, call 717-532-3040.

Reach us on the Internet: www.destinyimage.com.

ISBN 13 TP: 978-0-7684-5036-1
ISBN 13 eBook: 978-0-7684-5037-8
ISBN 13 HC: 978-0-7684-5039-2
ISBN 13 LP: 978-0-7684-5038-5

For Worldwide Distribution, Printed in the U.S.A.
1 2 3 4 5 6 7 8 / 23 22 21 20 19

ACKNOWLEDGMENTS

JOE

I want to thank my beautiful wife, Heidi, who is a blessing from God to me. I love you with all my heart. You have always been my best friend, constant companion, and confidant. Without you, not only would this book never have been written, but I wouldn't be alive today.

HEIDI

To my wonderful husband, Joe, who is not only my very best friend, but a faithful prayer warrior. You so unselfishly give of yourself to me personally and to our marriage. I have even yet much to glean from your example. You hold my heart and always will.

JOE & HEIDI

Thanks to our sons, Joey, Jonathan, and Joshua who have graciously shared us with others for all of their lives. You have grown up to be such fine godly men. And to Amanda, our amazing daughter-in-law, who is such a blessing and an answer to our prayers.

Thanks to our parents for giving us life, taking such good care of us, and encouraging us to follow our dreams. Because of you, we are.

Thanks to Joan Hunter who was instrumental in Joe's healing and encouraged us to write this book and to become ordained ministers of the Gospel of our Lord Jesus Christ. Without her love and constant friendship, our lives wouldn't have been the same.

Thanks to our good friends, Pastors Donna and Terry Wise, for patiently walking with us through Joe's healing and mentoring us into the possibilities in God beyond where we were spiritually. We are forever grateful.

Thanks to our friend Barbara Wentroble for her incredible leadership and the prophetic words she spoke over us. They are now coming true.

Thanks to our friends Jeff and Kim Brewer who encouraged us to write this book. Without Jeff's experience in writing and publishing you wouldn't be reading this today.

Thanks to Pastors Alex and Liz Barefoot, our pastors and our friends at Eastside Church. We are learning so much from you. Your passion for the Lord is truly refreshing.

Thanks to Randy Clark for being so compassionate and being humble enough to set us straight on healing.

This list would be endless, so to all of the people unnamed here who have been so instrumental in our lives—thank you for your love, prayers, and encouragement. May you be truly blessed.

And most of all, "thanks be to God, who gives us the victory through our Lord Jesus Christ" (1 Cor. 15:57).

In Him, everything is Yes and Amen!

CONTENTS

FOREWORD

I got an email one day asking for prayer. I knew in my heart and spirit that the woman was desperate. God said to call them (even though it was a holiday) and pray with them. When I called, I could hear screams in the background because of the intensity of the pain. I prayed, and as I prayed, very little relief came.

Then what?

And so this story unfolds...

How great is the grace and the healing power of our God! How wondrous are His ways! Few messages have the power to affect the lives of others more than a testimony of a miraculous healing experience.

Dr. Joe and Heidi Wadlinger's testimony of overcoming an incurable and life-threatening disease, which filled Joe with pain for many years, can change your life too. It was an experience that tested their love for each other as well as their faith in God. It drove them to seek God in a deeper way and led finally to Joe's complete healing.

Although most of the people I pray for are healed instantly, Joe received his over a period of time. He did not give up! He received prayer many times and sought God with tears until he was healed and whole. As his faith grew his healing progressed until all pain was gone and he could function normally. Joe and Heidi learned a great deal during this period of their lives, and in *Healed! God's Breakthrough Blueprint for Receiving and Releasing Miracles* they share that knowledge they gained during this painful odyssey with you. I heartily recommend you read their story and learn all you can from their experiences.

JOAN HUNTER
Author/Healing Evangelist
www.joanhunter.org

INTRODUCTION

Lord, we pray for everyone who reads this testimony. First of all we speak blessing over them in the name of Jesus. We ask as they read these words that You, by the power of the Holy Spirit, will guide them into all Your truth. That it will encourage every one of them to pursue You and Your Presence with their whole heart. And that the stories will challenge them to persevere for what Your Word says they can have through the salvation that was purchased by Your Son. That they will know that each one is Your favorite child and will have a renewed hope for things they have given up on. And that the lies of the enemy of our souls will be exposed and Your Word will prevail. We speak total wholeness of body, soul, spirit, and provision to each one of them in the mighty name of Jesus. Amen and amen!

—Dr. Joe and Heidi Wadlinger

JOE

"I think you should write a book about your testimony," Jeff said. We knew he was right. My wife Heidi and I had just met Jeff and his wife Kim. We were all there finishing our final requirements for ministerial ordination in Joan Hunter Ministries based in Tomball, Texas. In the Wednesday service the night before, Joan had asked Heidi and me to share the testimony of my healing to the over 200 people who were in attendance. After that, during almost every break, people were lining up to talk to us. Many were thanking us for sharing the process we had gone through for me to be whole. It had encouraged them to persevere for healing. Others wanted to know more details. Some wanted us to pray for them, their family, or their friends.

We knew our testimony had a very positive impact on those with whom we shared it, but this was the first time we had shared it with so many people at once, and the response was overwhelming. Jeff was encouraging me to write a book so that our story would affect many more people with whom we may never get to share our testimony face to face. But how was I supposed to do that? I only had some rudimentary knowledge about how to write and publish a book. I thought a book had to be at least 200 pages and that seemed to me to be a daunting task. So I looked at Jeff and said, "I don't know how to do that." He reassuringly replied, "But I do." We spent much of the time we had together discussing his knowledge of the publishing business, and the fact that he had written a number of books of his own. I knew then that God had put us together for His purposes. This book is the result of those kinds of divine connections. We will tell the story from both of our vantage points. There are wonderful lessons to be learned from not only me, who was physically afflicted, but also Heidi who had to take on a new role as my nurse, caregiver, and spiritual intercessor.

It is difficult to just start out telling you how God healed me from such a debilitating disease without giving you some background on our lives. The faithfulness of God has been so apparent through the years—and there have been so many, what we like to call, "God sightings" along the way—that we believe this history will give you a better understanding of the nature of God and how wonderfully personal He is.

The Greek word *sozo* is sometimes translated in the New Testament as "healed." An example is the woman with the issue of blood who was healed by Jesus.

> *But Jesus turned around, and when He saw her He said, "Be of good cheer, daughter; your faith has made you well [sozo]." And the woman was made well [sozo] from that hour* (Matthew 9:22).

Sozo means more than just to make well physically. Strong's says that sozo means "heal, preserve, save (self), do well, be (make) whole."

Here is an example of the word sozo being translated as "saved."

> *For God did not send His Son into the world to condemn the world, but that the world through Him might be saved [sozo]* (John 3:17).

So as we can see, when Jesus saved the world, He literally was making the world "whole" again. He came to make His children whole spiritually, mentally, emotionally, and physically, which includes our bodies as well as our finances. (See Second Corinthians 8:9.)

With that understanding we will start off with a short autobiography of our lives hitting some of the highlights that show how God is a personal God and interested in every aspect of our lives.

Chapter 1

BACKGROUND

JOE

I was born Joseph Allen Wadlinger in New Castle, Pennsylvania to my wonderful parents Joseph and Frances on Saint Patrick's Day in a snowstorm. My father barely got to the hospital in time. After he got over the shock of my cone shaped head, as a result of my time in the birth canal, he welcomed me into the family as their first child. My parents couldn't be any more different. My father, the eleventh of twelve children and the last boy of six, comes from a very German Catholic background. One of his sisters had even dedicated her life as a nun. My mother, on the other hand, comes from a Pentecostal Italian family where she was one of six and the middle girl of three.

My wonderful sister Deborah was born two and a half years later and our family was complete. My parents provided a warm, loving, and encouraging environment for us to grow up in. We moved to Kettering, Ohio when I was six years old and I spent my elementary school years there in a neighborhood full of children around my own age. Even though my family went to a Pentecostal church, I got saved that same year at Vacation Bible School in a friend's Methodist church. I remember very distinctly running up to my mother and saying, "Mommy, I just asked Jesus into my heart." I did all the typical things young boys do, and because my father was an engineer I developed a love for all kinds of things mechanical and electrical, especially computers, audio, and video.

We moved to Troy, Michigan when I was in seventh grade and I finished up my junior and senior high school years there. I was very involved in photography, drama, choir, and the honor society as well as being the head of the audiovisual department in my senior year. I was honored to be salutatorian of my high school class. I attended Wayne State University in Detroit where I graduated Phi Beta Kappa and Phi Lambda Upsilon with a degree in chemistry and went on to the medical school to earn my medical degree.

I met my wife Heidi in junior high school and she became one of my best friends. Early on we mostly dated other people because we really had little romantic interest in each other. We did date each other a few times and even went to the senior prom and many other important events together, but it never developed into anything lasting.

One day, in the summer between my first and second year of medical school, I was praying and asking the Lord about who I would marry one day. I had been praying for many years for that special woman whom God would reveal to me at a future date. I would pray that He would save her, fill her with His Holy Spirit, prepare her to be my wife, and also prepare me to be her husband.

This time, unexpectedly, He gave me an answer. He said, "You are to marry Heidi." His voice was as clear as if He was standing right there in the room talking to me. I didn't hear it audibly, but in my spirit it was clearer than even that. Immediately a love like I had never had for anyone else before sprang up inside of my heart and I knew that she was the one. As soon as I got back into town, I went straight to her house and asked her if we could start going out together. She said she was currently dating someone else. I was so sure of what God had spoken to me that I said, "Well, when you are through with him, I'll be here." Within a very short time we were dating, got engaged, and then married. On our wedding day we had known each other for over nine years.

After we had been married for a few years, I received my medical degree and we moved to Charlotte, North Carolina where I started my internship. About halfway through I realized that patient care wasn't where I was supposed to be and instead got a job in a large healthcare computer company that developed software for doctors' offices and hospitals. I knew in my heart that this was where God wanted me to be. I could use my medical knowledge and also my technical talents in this arena.

Meanwhile, Heidi and I wanted to have children. We had been trying for a long time and the wait was agonizing, especially for her. It seemed like everyone around us was getting pregnant but us. Maybe it was because I had always prayed that the Lord would only give us children who would serve Him. I asked that we would never lose even one of our descendants to the enemy. We continued praying and trusting God because we knew that children are a gift from the Lord and our inheritance. Once, during that time, we were offered a baby to adopt and were seriously considering it. We took it to the Lord and He said, "No, this one isn't yours." We knew at that point God had other plans in store.

One day while I was driving to the airport to fly out to California for a business trip, I stopped at a red light. Suddenly I had an open vision. In my arms was a little baby boy with blue eyes. This was a little strange because both Heidi and I have hazel-brown eyes, so blue eyes wouldn't be what I would have expected. I heard the Lord in my spirit say that this son would be like a Jeremiah and to name him such. Immediately I called Heidi at home and told her she was pregnant with a little boy with blue eyes. She said, "I am not! I know my own body and I would know if I was pregnant!" I knew by the hurt tone of her voice that she felt this was a cruel thing to say, raising her expectations without physical proof after all we had been through waiting on a child. But just like when God spoke to me about marrying her, I knew this was Him.

Later, after I had gotten to my hotel, I received a phone call. It was Heidi. "I just wanted to let you know that you were right," she said apologetically but with excitement, "I did a home pregnancy test and I'm pregnant!" That boy, with blue eyes, was our first son and we named him Joseph Jeremy. (In the King James Version of the New Testament in Matthew 27:9 it refers to Jeremiah as the prophet Jeremy.) Jeremiah was called the weeping prophet and Joey, as he likes to be called, has the most compassion for people of anyone in our family. Before our other two sons were born, the Lord would tell me that Heidi was pregnant before she knew, but it didn't come in a vision like that one. Our other two sons, who have brown eyes, are Jonathan David and Joshua Paul. All three are wonderful men who love the Lord. It is always better to wait on the Lord. Most often His perfect timing isn't ours.

After a number of years working for the healthcare computing company and another small computing company, two of my friends and I started our own business building data collection software for various industries. The Lord really blessed us, and at one time our company employed 21 people and did several million dollars in sales in our peak year. Due to the wisdom of the Holy Spirit, we were able to do for our customers what other companies had failed at.

> *If you need wisdom, ask our generous God, and he will give it to you. He will not rebuke you for asking* (James 1:5 NLT).

Whenever we needed revenue I would go to the Lord in prayer and He would answer. It used to be a joke between my business partner and me. He would say, "Joe, you can stop praying now, we have more work than we can handle."

HEIDI

I grew up as Heidi Anneliese Boden, the daughter of two German immigrant parents. My father Heinz came from a family of two boys and one girl. He contracted polio when he was a child and has had to deal with that physical challenge all his life. He taught me how to persevere and to never give up even in the hard times. He is a very strong man with strong convictions. When he married my mother, he adopted me and gave me his name. It wasn't until I was 23 years old that I knew about this because he has always treated me like his very own daughter. My mother Waltraud had one sister, who was my godmother, and a half-brother and a half-sister from my grandfather's first marriage. Wally, as my mother was called, grew up to become independent and self-reliant and was a very talented seamstress. My brother Hans was born one year after me and we lived in Michigan most of our lives.

I grew up loving music. My parents always had German music playing in our home. I learned to play the guitar when I was twelve and went on to learn piano and bass guitar. I sang everywhere—school, church, honors choir, ensembles, madrigals, and singing groups. My family was actively involved in community theater. My mother was very talented and made beautiful costumes. My father was gifted at electronics, stage lighting, and sound. My brother and I loved singing and acting. In high school I was involved in choir and many dramas. I even co-starred in my junior year in the musical *Oklahoma* and was the star of another musical in my senior year.

I met Joe in junior high and we became close and lasting friends in eighth grade because of algebra class. I was struggling to understand the math, unlike Joe who would correct the teacher's solutions to the problems that were written on the chalkboard. I asked if he would help me, and after that we would spend hours on the phone almost every night doing our algebra problems together. I said almost every night because on Wednesdays he went to church. That was very strange to me. I thought you only had to go to church on Sunday.

In our senior year Joe's sister Debbie asked me if I wanted to join their Christian singing group. The only Christian music I knew about sounded like funeral music. Fortunately, the music they were singing was contemporary Christian music. "Wow," I thought, "This is good, I'm in." They invited me to their church, which was a Pentecostal denomination, and as the service progressed I wondered what I had gotten myself into. People were raising their hands and singing, giving prophecies, and speaking in other languages in prayer. Joe and Debbie say that I actually looked very concerned and slid down in my seat. I couldn't wait to get out of there. But one thing kept me coming back. These people really seemed to believe in Jesus. For the first time in my life I asked Jesus to come into my life, was baptized in water, and filled with the Holy Spirit. Jesus has been my Lord ever since.

I was 19 years old and struggling with God's will for my life when I asked the Lord, "Am I supposed to stay single all my life or get married?" He said to me, "You are going to marry Joe Wadlinger." An immediate peace came over me and I put it out of my mind. We weren't even dating then. I didn't remember that the Lord had said that to me until He reminded me after Joe asked me to marry him.

At the time Joe and I started dating, the relationship I had with my parents was very strained. When I became a Christian, I think my mom and dad thought I had joined a cult. Their form of Christianity and mine were very different, so there was an attitude I had developed in that area that bordered on rebellion. This caused our communication to be contentious. Joe picked up on this and told me that if we were to continue our relationship, then I needed to humble myself and ask my parents to forgive me for that attitude.

One day when I was sitting at the kitchen table with my mom and dad, I told them how wrong I had been and asked for their forgiveness. Immediately it felt as if a giant wall between us had crumbled and mutual respect rose in its place. Communication became easier and our relationship grew in trust.

While Joe and I were still dating, my parents surprised me and said they had decided to move from Michigan and settle in the Carolinas. My father felt it would be better for his health. I was torn as to what I should do. Should I stay there in Michigan or go with them? I humbled myself, prayed for God to give my parents wisdom, and asked my mom and dad what they wanted me to do. "We think you have a future here with Joe," they said. "You should stay here."

Joe and I got married in his second year of medical school. I had been working as a dental technician and supported us through Joe's last years of school. When he decided to not become a practicing physician I was relieved. I really wasn't excited about being married to a doctor. At that time I had heard that many doctors' families suffered from long work hours, absence from home, and stress.

I continued working even after our first son Joey was born because we needed the extra income. I never said anything to Joe, but I was becoming increasingly grieved that I had to leave Joey at the babysitter's house as I put in a full work week at the dental laboratory. I started asking the Lord that when Joey reached the age of two He would let me quit my job and be a stay-at-home mom.

One day, just before Joey was two years old, Joe said, "I have been thinking. I believe I'm now making enough money at my job that when Joey turns two you can quit your job and stay home with him." Tears started to well up in my eyes. The Lord had heard my prayers and had answered them exactly how I had asked Him. Joe had no clue as to my desire or the time frame I had asked God for. We were amazed at the goodness of God and how He had orchestrated everything to make this happen.

God has always provided for us both naturally and supernaturally. One story I like to tell is a period in our lives when we were getting checks and money almost every week from all sorts of unexpected places. Joe would walk in and say, "Here's another one," and we would laugh in amazement. When the checks stopped, we had tens of thousands of dollars in our savings account. We were dreaming up things that we could do with the money. We could put a new room on the house, go on a trip, or give it away. We prayed and God said, "No, put it away and keep it for a year, and if you still have it, you are free to do what you want with it." Little did we know, but He did, that Joe wouldn't be taking a salary from his company for almost two and a half years. We lived off of that blessing for all of that time. When his salary started again we had about $200 left in that savings account. The verse in Matthew 6:8 where Jesus says, "For your Father knows the things you have need of before you ask Him," became very real to us and is still a word we live by today.

Joe has always been a strong spiritual leader in our home. That allowed me to relax under that spiritual umbrella and not do a lot of praying and Bible studying on my own. Even though my faith was strong, I wasn't prepared for what was to come next.

Chapter 2

THE PAIN BEGINS

JOE

I had always been a very healthy adult. But in 2004, that began to change. I was spending late evenings at work building our company and programming long hours continuously each day. I began to have problems with my lower back, which caused sciatic nerve pain to radiate down my right leg. That year, the pain had become so severe that I could only work half days and had to come home and lie down as the pain throbbed relentlessly. I went to see a neurosurgeon who diagnosed that I had a bulging disk between my fourth and fifth lumbar vertebrae.

He asked me what kind of chair I sat in to program at work and what my posture was like. I told him that I sat in a high back executive chair and kind of slid down and slouched forming a "C" with my back. He showed me the MRI. Because of my posture I had deformed my back and made it susceptible to this kind of injury. He gave me two options—physical therapy or surgery. My father had had surgery when he was about my age for a similar thing and it fixed the problem, so I opted for the surgery.

After the surgery the pain diminished significantly and I went home to recover, but I made a major mistake that being a doctor I should have known not to make. I felt guilty just staying home and allowing myself to recover so I got a laptop, laid in our big leather recliner on a heating pad, and starting programming again for work. The heating pad felt good, but by just lying there my back muscles deteriorated instead of strengthened and my spine didn't have the benefit of exercise to strengthen the bones, surrounding muscles, and ligaments to keep the same thing from happening again. I had just compounded the problem.

Less than a year later, after working out on a stair stepper exercise machine, I felt a searing pain worse than I ever had before going from my lower back to my big toe on my right foot. I had to lay perfectly straight on my back. If I bent at all the pain felt like someone had clamped the two leads of an arc welder from my back to my foot. The pain was so bad that my father, my wife, and my sons had to make a stretcher and carry me into the neurosurgeon's office. He took one look and sent me straight over to the hospital for emergency surgery.

Just before the surgery I had an MRI. The technician said that the disc had "blown out" and a large piece had lodged in my spinal canal and was pressing on my spinal column causing the pain. The surgery was successful and the searing pain went away. The neurosurgeon said the disk fragments were among the largest he had ever seen. One was about the size of a quarter. But I still hadn't learned my lesson and continued programming from the recliner with a heating pad on my lower spine.

I never returned to normal and there was still weakness and mild pain in my back, leg, and gluteal muscles. Somehow, around this time, I had come down with walking pneumonia that was undiagnosed for almost a year. When it was finally found and treated, it had so drained my body that I became severely depressed. Not remembering that it takes several months to get over the effects of pneumonia, I asked my personal physician to put me on antidepressants. I reacted terribly with incredible anxiety and strange sensations in my body, but I was afraid to get off of the medication completely even though the amount I was taking was minimal.

I went back to my neurosurgeon complaining about the residual pain. He said that he wouldn't do another surgery but would send me to a hospital-based pain clinic for evaluation. The physician at the pain clinic happened to be the head doctor there. He recommended that they inject my spine with a corticosteroid medication that might help alleviate my pain. The procedure technically went well and he was pleased. I went home to bed with an ice pack on my back as the doctor had prescribed. Suddenly, it felt like someone took a hot poker and thrust it into my lower back. It was pain like I had never experienced before in my entire life. I knew there was a problem and I began weeping and cried out, "What have I done?"

The pain began extending from my lower spine and grew to encompass my entire right leg. It was like having someone pour hot lava, not only on my skin, but deep inside my back and in the muscles, nerves, and bones of my leg. There was no comfortable position that I could put myself in. Sitting was the worst. I had to stand to eat, but I had to do that quickly and lie down or the pain would overwhelm me. The position where I had the least pain was lying on my stomach, so we purchased a massage table so I could do that more comfortably.

We called the doctor and went back to the pain clinic as soon as we could. When the doctor saw me he said, with tears welling up in his eyes, "Oh my, I am so sorry, I did this to you!" Little did we know that 1 in about 3,000 patients can have this kind of reaction to corticosteroid injections in the spine.

This is what the site DrugLib.com says about this particular medication: (My notations are in brackets and italics are added for emphasis).

> Warning: This product contains benzyl alcohol, which is potentially *toxic* when administered locally to *neural tissue*. [Neural tissue is the brain, spinal cord, and nerves.]
>
> Adverse Reactions: Intrathecal/Epidural: *Arachnoiditis*, bowel/bladder dysfunction, headache, meningitis, parapareisis/paraplegia, seizures, *sensory disturbances*. [Epidural is basically the space around the spinal cord.]

Even though physicians use this medication to inject into the spinal canal to reduce inflammation, it is an "off-label" usage. This means that physicians have found it effective even though the FDA hasn't specifically approved it for that use. Thousands upon thousands of people have had this procedure done with no adverse effects. I happened to be one of the unfortunate few.

HEIDI

I could see that the doctor, also a Christian, was so remorseful and was probably wondering if we were going to bring some kind of a lawsuit. I turned to him and said, "Doctor, we know this wasn't your fault and we don't hold you responsible. We just want you to know that." The expression of relief on his face was tangible and from that moment on he always made himself available to us.

JOE

I was still hoping that the doctors would find an answer. We went back to the pain clinic often and I begged the doctors to help me. I had multiple MRIs to see what might be wrong. Even though my neurosurgeon was unwilling to do another back surgery, I was desperate. I knew that I had some relief before and maybe, just maybe, I would get it again. Another neurosurgeon had mercy on me and scheduled a third back surgery to remove any scar tissue that may be impinging on my nerves and causing the pain. After the surgery the doctor told Heidi, "The surgery went well. There was a lot of scar tissue in there, but I got all of it out. I believe he is going to feel much better." Unfortunately, the surgery didn't seem to help at all and the pain only got worse. We were running out of options.

Among the many MRIs I had at this time, there was one that identified the real problem. The radiologist reported that it looked like I might have an incurable condition called arachnoiditis. This finding was dismissed by my pain specialist. When I brought it to his attention, he said that he didn't believe that diagnosis was correct. But as I detailed above, this is one of the rare adverse reactions to injecting corticosteroids into the spine.

From the NIH.gov website (italics are added for emphasis):

What is arachnoiditis?

Arachnoiditis describes a pain disorder caused by the inflammation of the arachnoid, one of the membranes that surround and protect the nerves of the spinal cord. The arachnoid can become inflamed because of an irritation from *chemicals*, infection from bacteria or viruses, as the result of direct injury to the spine, chronic compression of spinal nerves, or *complications from spinal surgery or other invasive spinal procedures*. Inflammation can sometimes lead to the formation of *scar tissue and adhesions*, which *cause the spinal nerves to "stick" together*. If arachnoiditis begins to interfere with the function of one or more of these nerves, it can cause a number of symptoms, including *numbness, tingling, and a characteristic stinging and burning pain in the lower back or legs*. Some people with arachnoiditis will have *debilitating muscle cramps, twitches, or spasms*. It may also affect bladder, bowel, and sexual function. In severe cases, arachnoiditis may cause paralysis of the lower limbs.

Is there any treatment?

Arachnoiditis remains a difficult condition to treat, and long-term outcomes are unpredictable. Most treatments for arachnoiditis are focused on pain relief and the improvement of symptoms that impair daily function. A regimen of pain management, physiotherapy, exercise, and psychotherapy is often recommended. Surgical intervention is controversial since the outcomes are generally poor and provide only short-term relief.

What is the prognosis?

Arachnoiditis is a disorder that causes *chronic pain and neurological deficits* and *does not improve significantly with treatment*. Surgery may only provide temporary relief. The outlook for someone with arachnoiditis is complicated by the fact that the disorder has no predictable pattern or severity of symptoms (http://www.ninds.nih.gov/disorders/arachnoiditis/arachnoiditis.htm).

HEIDI

The doctors had tried everything to correct what they thought was the problem. They were already trying medications to reduce or mask the pain. It seemed like every medication they tried either didn't work at all or caused side effects Joe couldn't tolerate. The next treatment suggestion was to put a programmable nerve stimulator in Joe's spine to try to cover the pain up with a different sensation. A new doctor had come to run the pain clinic. He was world renowned in the placement and management of nerve stimulators. He was sure this would be the answer to our dilemma. This stimulator had worked for thousands of others with intractable nerve pain. I told Joe that I wasn't in favor of this operation. Something inside of me felt like it wouldn't work for him, but he was determined that this was the only thing he hadn't tried and because of his desperation I agreed to let the doctor put it in.

During the first surgery Joe was blissfully in sedated sleep. Only one wire was placed and Joe felt it didn't give him any relief. The doctor decided to do another operation to put in a second wire. This time he did it with Joe awake and with minimal anesthesia so he could try to place the lead where Joe said the pain was most severe. Joe said that he could feel the wire being pushed up his spinal canal to its final position. The feeling was extremely uncomfortable and even eerie. But even after those two surgeries to place the stimulator wires in his spine, Joe wasn't to be one of the successes. Instead of reducing the pain, it just added a feeling on top of the pain that felt like a mild pulsating electrical shock. Joe was extremely disillusioned and became even more depressed. We finally asked the surgeon to remove the stimulator and the wires, because they weren't doing any good, which took a third surgery.

After this surgery the doctor came into the recovery room and took me aside. "I think you need to take him to a psychiatrist," he said. I was indignant. "You don't even know this man," I said,

"This isn't at all who he is. This is all a reaction to the pain and medications." We never went back to the pain clinic to see this doctor again.

Chapter 3

IT GETS WORSE

JOE

The next two years were a living hell for me and a nightmare for Heidi and my family. The pain only got worse, and because I was in bed most of the day I was losing muscle size and strength. My ligaments grew weaker and my spine wasn't being supported properly. This just aggravated the burning pain and my joints would go out of place and become inflamed, adding more pain in other parts of my body. The original pain doctor tried me on NSAIDs, oral corticosteroids, narcotics, antidepressants, muscle relaxers, and many other types of medications. He even tried some medications that they give to cancer patients to ease their agony, but nothing touched the intractable pain. Many of the medications caused nausea, heart palpitations, anxiety, nightmares, depression, and other psychological and physical symptoms. I was continually depressed and my physician was trying everything he knew to do, but to no avail.

My body was constantly focused on the excruciating pain because it never let up. Just imagine that you just smashed your thumb with a hammer. In that instant you would drop the hammer, grit your teeth, and grab your thumb tightly in the other hand. All you would care about is the thumb and the pain. Every thought in your brain would be directed toward that pain. If someone were to ask you even a simple question in that moment, like "What is 2+2?" you probably wouldn't be able to answer or even care. It's all about the pain. Normally that intenseness only lasts for a little while, and then reduces into a dull ache and eventually goes away in a few days. Now imagine if nerve pain more intense than that encompassed your entire lower body and never went away. If you can image that, then you will understand, in some measure, what I was going through.

Any situation that took even a small amount of brainpower would literally cause the pain to increase in intensity, as my mind would have to give up focusing on mentally managing the pain to focus on something else. My stress hormones were depleted and my brain felt the brunt of trying to manage everything by itself.

I remember one situation that is a good example of what would happen on a regular basis. It was tax time. I had been doing my own taxes since I was a teenager and even though it was intense and stressful each year, it was just a marathon session and got done. This year it was different. I had to direct my wife and my mother to collect all the paperwork, organize it, and then enter it into the computer tax program that I normally used. I would get up out of bed, go into the room where they were working, lie down again, and then guide them through the process for about an hour, maybe two. Then my brain would exhaust, my stress and pain would go through the roof, I would excuse myself with tears in my eyes and tell them I needed to go lie down again to allow my brain to return to managing the pain for a while, and then I could come back. That process happened over and over again until it was finally done. It seemed to me to take forever, and after that I had to allow my body to recover for a long time. Any decision-making was like this and the big decisions took an even larger toll.

Because of my condition I could no longer work, even at home. Fortunately my business had purchased long-term disability insurance, which I qualified for, and after that ran out, Social Security quickly put me on disability. Usually it takes a long time to get approved for Social Security disability, but because arachnoiditis is so severe, and because the doctor wrote a report to them that said that I would never be able to work again, there was no resistance at all. Unfortunately the amount of money I received from that wasn't enough to support our high medical expenditures, medical insurance, and the expenses for a family of five. My parents graciously and lovingly picked up the slack and supported us both financially and physically. The Lord even impressed on an anonymous couple in our church to give us $1,000! The Lord Who Provides, Jehovah Jireh, never failed us and we were never in lack. Praise His name.

The people of my church rallied around us in prayer, especially in the first months. But as time went on I think they ran out of answers as to how to pray for me. A few were faithful to visit whenever they could with encouragement. Some said that I was like Job and God had put me through this so that He could show His sovereignty. Some said that we didn't have enough faith. A few suggested that I just "pull myself up by my bootstraps" and just go about my day as though I was already healed and just ignore the pain. But most didn't know what to do and eventually I felt lonely and abandoned. Part of that was my own fault because most of the time I didn't even feel well enough to have anyone visit and encouraged Heidi to tell them not to come, even if they were going to pray for me.

I began to feel abandoned by God too. Didn't He see me? Didn't He know I was in so much pain? Why was I singled out for this? I was a better Christian than most people I knew. Hey, I had even been a deacon and an elder. I had taught Sunday school for years. I had been faithful to always pay my tithes and give offerings. I went to church almost every time the doors were open and probably was at more services than the pastor. Didn't God know that? I started saving up pills to commit suicide and I didn't even care what God thought about it. I mean, God had abandoned me anyway. Why did I think I would even make it into Heaven? I must not be good enough to be healed. Obviously I was in a deep depression and my ability to trust God had gone the way of my pain.

It had gotten so bad that I wouldn't let Heidi leave the house. The pain would spike many times during the day especially when the weather changed and the barometer would either rise or fall. She could tell you when it was about to rain because the pain would get so bad that I would put a pillow over my face and scream. I was so afraid that I wouldn't let her go out of the house unless it was on my terms. I would say, "I'm going to lie in bed until 11 a.m. and pretend you are here. Then I will call out to you and I will expect you to come. If you leave, please don't let me know. Just make sure you are back by eleven or I don't know what I will do."

HEIDI

When I was home, I would help Joe out to the massage table where I would spend hours massaging his muscles to release the spasms and reduce the pain. Once a week Joe's mother would come over and stay with him while I ran errands. There were several times she had to call me to come home because she couldn't stand watching him suffer. I had to do all of this and take care of three sons, one dog, and an entire household as well. I felt trapped, but I never let on. When Joe would lose hope I would say, "If I have to throw you over my shoulder and carry you across the finish line we are going to see you healed."

I continued to encourage myself in the Lord. I cannot count the number of times he would look pitifully into my eyes and say, "You won't leave me will you?" My answer was always firm and resolute. "When we married," I would proclaim, "I took wedding vows that said for richer or poorer and in sickness and in health. I meant them then and I still mean them now, so I'm not going anywhere. You are stuck with me." I was resolute, even though there were many times I felt like just getting in a car and driving away for good.

What was even more significant to me was not having Joe's spiritual leadership anymore. He was unsure and wavering. The medications were taking their toll on his brain. Most times he couldn't even put together a complete sentence. He was forgetful and repeated himself all the time. And he questioned what he had believed about God all of his life. It was now up to me to take the lead and spend time with God for all of us. My family was suffering, and if I didn't get direction from the Lord, it was going to be in shambles. I spent more time in the Word and in prayer than I ever had in my entire life. I would get up early and stay up late trying to find the answers we needed.

There were times Joe and I would pray 8, 10, or even 12 hours a day. We would speak in tongues for hours. We played worship music all day long and worshiped as much as we were able. We read the Bible all the time. We had Scripture verses taped everywhere and prayer cloths pinned to his clothes and pillowcase. Joe would tell me that it seemed like God didn't care or wasn't even there. He started to think that he had believed a lie about God and had been brainwashed by the church. He was asking, "Was God real, or if He was, did He even care about us?"

I started to wonder if we were missing something. My faith was still strong. "I think we should throw out everything we know about healing and start from scratch," I said to Joe. "Let's start with what the Bible says and then start reading books from people who experienced the healing power of God in their lives and ministries." His mother purchased us a subscription to a satellite network that featured Christian TV channels and we started watching every healing evangelist program we could find. I believe the Spirit of God guided us in which programs to watch that would encourage us that healing was real.

The biggest breakthroughs were from the books we found on healing that had been written decades before. These men and women were the pioneers in bringing back healing to the church.

Before their time (and even today) there were those who said that the kind of healing we see in the Bible died out with the apostles. They said that God is sovereign and He heals whom He wants, when He wants, but our direct prayers have little to do with whether someone is healed or not. These pioneers challenged that theology and saw incredible miracles by using the authority that Christ Jesus has given to us.

> *And the glory which You gave Me I have given them, that they may be one just as We are one: I in them, and You in Me; that they may be made perfect in one, and that the world may know that You have sent Me, and have loved them as You have loved Me* (John 17:22-23).

These pioneers laid hands on the sick and saw them miraculously recover. Many of them came out of the early Pentecostal movement that started with the Azusa Street revival. The walls of their meetings were lined with wheelchairs and crutches, casts and braces. Jesus' command for us to "heal the sick, raise the dead, cast out devils and cleanse lepers" was taken seriously and showed the Kingdom of Heaven really was at hand. Everyone who came to Jesus was healed and He gave us that authority and they believed it and demonstrated it.

One of the books that we read and led us to many others was *God's Generals* by Roberts Liardon. In its pages we read about those people and "why they succeeded and why some failed." We read about John Alexander Dowie, Maria Woodworth-Etter, Evan Roberts, Charles Parham, William J. Seymour (of the Azusa Street revival), John G. Lake (our personal favorite), Aimee Semple

McPherson, Smith Wigglesworth, Kathryn Kuhlman, and many more. Granted, none of these people were perfect, and they had their struggles, and some ended very poorly, but they were seeing people, like Joe and worse, healed!

We began devouring these resources. I read to Joe from these books and also the verses from the Bible that spoke about healing. I walked him out to the massage table and worked on him while we watched people on television teaching on healing and the testimonies of people who were being healed. We had entered a whole new realm. We had never heard of most of these people before and we marveled that after all our years in Christianity this had been hidden from us. A treasure that had been buried was now found and we were digging it up.

Like I said previously, one of the ministers who was our personal favorite to read about was John G. Lake. He died in 1935, but his legacy lives on in a ministry called "Healing Rooms." While he was alive his healing rooms documented over 100,000 healings. He was a dynamic man and gave up a lucrative career to pursue God and minister His healing power all over the world. Then there was Smith Wigglesworth, a plumber by trade, who not only saw incredible healings but raised people from the dead by the power of God. This only egged us on that healing was possible for Joe and we started to look for modern-day people through whom true miracles were happening.

Reading about John G. Lake started me thinking a lot about the healing rooms. While lying in bed one night I had an urge to look it up on the internet. Lo and behold, they were still in existence today and there were some in our area. We started going to one in Charlotte and the people there were so encouraging and prayed for Joe with such compassion. Because Joe couldn't sit without pain, I would load him into the back seat of the car where he could lie down until we got there. Then I would carry in an exercise mat and he would lie on it while we prayed and believed God. I can't say that anything physical happened at that time, but our faith got considerably stronger and Joe was much encouraged because of that.

Because it was such an incredible struggle for Joe to go to the healing rooms, he wouldn't let me take him there as much as I would have liked. They had a healing school and I decided I needed to go. Joe agreed. These people knew things that I needed to know. In my conversations with the people at the healing rooms in Charlotte, I heard about a ministry in Redding, California. Bethel Church was that place, and the national head of the Healing Rooms Ministries, Cal Pierce, had been an elder and a board member there. The senior pastor, Bill Johnson, really believes in healing and is a dynamic teacher of God's Word. I looked him up on the internet and we started watching him preach and tell numerous stories of people being healed, not only through him, but through the leaders and even the members of his church. The testimonies were amazing as people with almost every type of disease imaginable were being healed and restored. I remember Joe saying to me, "Do you think that those healings are real?" Joe needed something to hang on to and he needed it to be real. We called the church and the youth pastor prayed for us and said they would add Joe to their prayer list. We considered going there, but the trip would have been too much for Joe to handle.

I realized through these encounters that the healing power of God hadn't gone out with the apostles. It was real and it was happening in many places on a regular basis by the power of prayer. And there was a difference in the prayers. When these people prayed, they did it with authority. They didn't ask God to heal the person; they spoke to the disease or infirmity with authority and commanded what they wanted. This was new to us. Instead of saying something like, "Father, I ask You to heal Joe's back in the name of Jesus," they would say, "In the name of Jesus, I command this back to be healed. Pain and inflammation go! Nerves, vertebrae, muscles, and discs be made whole. Body, line up with the Word of God!" Wow, I could never remember anyone praying like that. They prayed as though they had the authority to heal in the name of Jesus. And it was working.

JOE

We started searching for healing in the Word of God. How did Jesus heal? How did the disciples heal? And you know what we found? They did it the same way. As we studied, we couldn't find even one place in the New Testament where Jesus, the apostles, or anyone else ever asked the Father to do the healing. They healed using the power and authority given by the Father to Jesus, who in turn gave it to them.

Here are some examples from Jesus:

The Madman at Capernaum (Mark 1:23-27)

> Now there was a man in their synagogue with an unclean spirit. And he cried out, saying, "Let us alone! What have we to do with You, Jesus of

Nazareth? Did You come to destroy us? I know who You are—the Holy One of God!"

But Jesus rebuked him, saying, "Be quiet, and come out of him!" And when the unclean spirit had convulsed him and cried out with a loud voice, he came out of him. Then they were all amazed, so that they questioned among themselves, saying, "What is this? What new doctrine is this? For with authority He commands even the unclean spirits, and they obey Him."

Peter's mother-in law (Matthew 8:14-17)

Now when Jesus had come into Peter's house, He saw his wife's mother lying sick with a fever. So He touched her hand, and the fever left her. And she arose and served them.

When evening had come, they brought to Him many who were demon-possessed. And He cast out the spirits with a word, and healed all who were sick, that it might be fulfilled which was spoken by Isaiah the prophet, saying: "He Himself took our infirmities and bore our sicknesses."

The Leper (Matthew 8:1-3)

When He had come down from the mountain, great multitudes followed Him. And behold, a leper came and worshiped Him, saying, "Lord, if You are willing, You can make me clean." Then Jesus put out

His hand and touched him, saying, "I am willing; be cleansed." Immediately his leprosy was cleansed.

Here are some examples from the disciples:

Success of the Seventy (Luke 10:8-9, 17)

Whatever city you enter, and they receive you, eat such things as are set before you. And heal the sick there, and say to them, "The kingdom of God has come near to you."

Then the seventy returned with joy, saying, "Lord, even the demons are subject to us in Your name."

Notice they said "us."

Man at the Gate Beautiful (Acts 3:6-8 NIV)

Then Peter said, "Silver or gold I do not have, but what I do have I give you. In the name of Jesus Christ of Nazareth, walk." Taking him by the right hand, he helped him up, and instantly the man's feet and ankles became strong. He jumped to his feet and began to walk.

Notice he said "I" twice.

Aeneas Healed (Acts 9:33-35)

There he found a certain man named Aeneas, who had been bedridden eight years and was paralyzed. And Peter said to him, "Aeneas, Jesus the Christ heals you. Arise and make your bed." Then he arose immediately. So all who dwelt at Lydda and Sharon saw him and turned to the Lord.

Tabitha Raised from the Dead (Acts 9:36-41)

At Joppa there was a certain disciple named Tabitha, which is translated Dorcas. This woman was full of good works and charitable deeds which she did. But it happened in those days that she became sick and died. When they had washed her, they laid her in an upper room. And since Lydda was near Joppa, and the disciples had heard that Peter was there, they sent two men to him, imploring him not to delay in coming to them. Then Peter arose and went with them.

When he had come, they brought him to the upper room. And all the widows stood by him weeping, showing the tunics and garments which Dorcas had made while she was with them. But Peter put them all out, and knelt down and prayed. And turning to the body he said, "Tabitha, arise." And she opened her eyes, and when she saw Peter she sat up. Then he gave her his hand and lifted her up; and when he had called the saints and widows, he presented her alive.

Notice that Peter prayed first. I believe that Peter knew that she was with the Lord and was asking God if He really wanted her to come back to the earth before he took authority over death. Take notice that it was after Peter prayed that he turned toward the body and spoke the command for her to arise. There are numerous examples of praying with authority like this in the New Testament, and I challenge you to study them for yourself.

So if the Lord and His disciples prayed that way, shouldn't we pray that way also? This was changing how we prayed. But another revelation was making its way into our theology. Look at Matthew 8:16. It states, "and healed all who were sick." See the word all? It also appears in other verses (see Matt. 4:24; 12:15; Luke 4:40; 6:19).

It says all who came to Him were healed. He never denied anyone healing. He never told them to wait for another time (although some were healed as they went). He never said they were suffering physical sickness as an example to others of how to suffer. He never told them He wouldn't heal them because their faith wasn't strong enough. In fact, He healed people with much faith, little faith, mother's faith, father's faith, friends' faith, master's faith, and even just His faith. It doesn't say everyone was healed, but it does say all those who came to Him were.

Jesus said, "He who has seen Me has seen the Father" (John 14:9), and that "He [Jesus] is the image of the invisible God" (Col. 1:15)

Jesus never put sickness or disease on anyone, so the argument that God puts diseases on His people for some divine purpose is recognized for what it really is—another lie of the enemy. Jesus only did what He saw His Father doing.

The next revelation for us was that there are instantaneous miracles and then there are healings. There is an example in the New Testament where people were healed as they went. In fact, it was about this time that the Lord told Heidi that my healing wasn't going to be an instantaneous miracle but a progressive healing over time. Of course, I didn't want to hear that. I wanted a miracle now. I didn't want to be in this excruciating pain one day longer. He told her it would be this way so I would learn how to stay healthy and not "lose my healing." I think it would be good at this point to define that term. I don't believe that we actually "lose" our healing, but if we don't do what is necessary to keep our bodies healthy and our relationship with the Lord strong, the same thing or worse can come back. In Matthew 12, Jesus says:

> *When an unclean spirit goes out of a man, he goes through dry places, seeking rest, and finds none. Then he says, "will return to my house from which I came." and when he comes, he finds it empty, swept, and put in order. Then he goes and takes with him seven other spirits more wicked than himself, and they enter and dwell there; and the last state of that man is worse than the first* (Matthew 12:43-45).

I believe He meant that once that unclean spirit was gone, if the man didn't fill that place in his life with the Holy Spirit, he was putting up a "vacancy" sign, and that thing would come back worse than it was before.

In John 5 Jesus heals a man from a sickness he suffered from for 38 years. Afterward He finds the man and tells him, "See you have been made well. Sin no more, lest a worse thing come upon you" (John 5:14).

I have personally witnessed people who have been healed, but didn't "maintain" their healing and it came back, sometimes worse.

A good example of people in the New Testament who didn't get healed instantly is found in Luke 17. It is the story of the ten lepers.

Now it happened as He went to Jerusalem that He passed through the midst of Samaria and Galilee. Then as He entered a certain village, there met Him ten men who were lepers, who stood afar off. And they lifted up their voices and said, "Jesus, Master, have mercy on us!"

So when He saw them, He said to them, "Go, show yourselves to the priests." And so it was that as they went, they were cleansed (Luke 17:11-14).

Note: If Jesus sent them from Galilee to the priests in Jerusalem, it could have been over 60 miles and a several-day journey. How far had they gotten before they noticed they were healed? This may partly explain why only one returned to thank Him.

See the words "as they went, they were cleansed." Jesus' authority had healed them, but they needed to be obedient and go show themselves to the priests. They all had the faith to go at His Word, and as they went they noticed that they were healed. Heidi was told by the Holy Spirit that this was what was going to happen to me. I was going to be healed, as Heidi likes to say, "As I was 'wenting.'"

Another example of a related principle can be found in Mark 8.

Then He came to Bethsaida; and they brought a blind man to Him, and begged Him to touch him. So He took the blind man by the hand and led him out of the town. And when He had spit on his eyes and put His hands on him, He asked him if he saw anything. And he looked up and said, "I see men like trees, walking." Then He put His hands on his eyes

*again and made him look up. And he was restored
and saw everyone clearly* (Mark 8:22-25).

Jesus prayed for the man twice. This was Jesus. Why did He
have to pray twice? Was this harder than raising Lazarus from the
dead? He only had to command that once. No, I believe Jesus was
demonstrating a principle for us—that healing is ours and we have
to see it that way. If we don't see complete healing the first time, we
need to keep praying and not give up until we get what we know is
ours through His sacrifice.

Jesus illustrates this principle through a parable He told to His
disciples in Luke 18:

> *Then He spoke a parable to them, that men always
> ought to pray and not lose heart, saying: "There was
> in a certain city a judge who did not fear God nor
> regard man. Now there was a widow in that city; and
> she came to him, saying, 'Get justice for me from my
> adversary.' And he would not for a while; but after-
> ward he said within himself, 'Though I do not fear
> God nor regard man, yet because this widow troubles
> me I will avenge her, lest by her continual coming she
> weary me.'"*
>
> *Then the Lord said, "Hear what the unjust judge
> said. And shall God not avenge His own elect who
> cry out day and night to Him, though He bears long
> with them? I tell you that He will avenge them speed-
> ily. Nevertheless, when the Son of Man comes, will
> He really find faith on the earth?"* (Luke 18:1-8)

The principle is stated in the first verse. I like to put it this way: He told them this parable so they would keep praying and not become discouraged or quit until they got their answer. He says that God will avenge (make right the situation) as we keep crying out to Him. He is equating this persistence with faith.

I believe these insights are keys. Too many times we become disheartened if we don't get our answer immediately or within a short period of time. We aren't promised instantaneous answers, but He will always answer us, and in the meantime He will be there with us in the struggle.

The Lord says to us:

> *When he calls on me, I will answer; I will be with him in trouble and rescue him and honor him* (Psalm 91:15 TLB).

As Alex Barefoot, lead pastor of Eastside Church in Charlotte, North Carolina likes to say, "We have been saved, we are being saved, and we will be saved." Well, because salvation includes healing, we can say, "We have been healed, we are being healed, and we will be healed."

Chapter 4

NEW HOPE ARISES

HEIDI

By now it was early 2008 and I heard about an outpouring of healing that was happening in Florida. The senior pastor of Ignited Church had asked a young healing evangelist to come and hold revival meetings for his congregation. People began to be healed in the services, and soon the revival was attracting people from all over the world with as many as up to 10,000 people in attendance.

Joe and I began to watch this amazing outpouring of healing and restoration on the internet and on television. The preaching and miracles confirmed what we had already been reading and watching at other churches, but the numbers of people healed were staggering. Joe would ask me many times, "Do you think those healings are real?" and, "Do you think I could be healed?" I wanted to take Joe to those meetings. We even had relatives who lived in the area. But Joe was in no condition to make that kind of trip. Day after day we watched in amazement and yearned to see that kind of thing happen in our lives. Then one day as we watched, we heard that the evangelist was coming to Concord, a town no more than 30 minutes from our home. Pastors Donna and Terry Wise from Impact Church had stepped out in faith and rented Cabarrus Arena. I decided we were going no matter what.

The evening came and we decided to get there early. I put Joe into the car with a mat and a walking stick. When we got to the arena there were hundreds of people there already. They were letting people inside in batches because there was a large crowd wanting to get in and only a limited number of seats. We were some of the fortunate ones who got inside. The event center, where the evangelist was going to be speaking, can hold about 8,000 people with overflow seating. By the time the event started, the arena was full. Reports said that about 5,000 people were turned away and there was a traffic jam of around 2,000 cars that formed a parking lot on the highway leading to the arena. Joe lay on the floor on his mat and couldn't even see the stage.

The evangelist spoke and called for people with specific diseases to come to the stage so he could pray for them. He didn't mention Joe's condition so we waited. At the end of the meeting they formed a healing "tunnel" for people to pass through as the evangelist and his leaders laid hands on them and prayed. There was no way Joe would be able to wait in that long line, so I asked someone to take a cloth and have the evangelist anoint it with oil so

I could place it upon Joe for healing. That night many were healed, but Joe didn't see any change in his condition. He went home disappointed and it just reinforced his feeling that he wasn't going to be healed. It was a setback for us, but I still knew that God is Jehovah Rapha, the Lord Our Healer, and that Joe was going to be healed. It just wasn't at this event.

One of the great things about the Florida services being televised and also online was that they not only broadcast the nightly meetings from Florida, but also many different meetings and workshops that were happening during the day by other ministers. One of these ministers was a lady healing evangelist by the name of Joan Hunter. Her parents, Charles and Frances Hunter, went all over the world holding healing meetings and were known as "The Happy Hunters."

Joan had traveled and ministered with her parents for many years. They were getting older and not traveling much anymore, so Joan had taken over that part of the ministry. When we listened to her teaching and watched how she ministered healing to people, we were amazed at the stark difference in ministry style from what we had seen before. There were no theatrics or loud shouting. She just asked the person what they needed, and then with calm but assured authority spoke to the infirmity and commanded it to do what she wanted in the name of Jesus. She didn't even close her eyes and told the sick person to keep theirs open too. "If you close your eyes, you may miss seeing your healing," she would say. I felt what she really meant was to throw away the trappings of what you have erroneously been taught about healing and embrace what the Bible really teaches. And the results were amazing. We saw more people get healed, right there on television, when she prayed for them than we had seen anywhere else.

Joe was very encouraged by what he saw, but he would still ask me, "Do you think that's real? Are those people really getting healed? Do you think I can be healed too?" Joan only did a few sessions at the church in Florida, but they would replay these sessions on the internet and TV several times a week for many weeks. It lifted Joe's faith so much that every time they would rebroadcast it, I would go into the bedroom and say, "Come on, Joan is on TV." Joe would struggle through the pain, get out of bed, walk to the massage table, lie down, and watch Joan again.

One particularly bad day for Joe—and there were many—my parents came from Florida to visit us. Joe told me to apologize to them for him because he wasn't feeling up to seeing anyone. This was a typical occurrence many times when people would come to the house. It happened to be Labor Day and I believe the Lord directed me to email Joan that day. I had never contacted her before, so she didn't know who we were. I emailed her about Joe's condition, asked her to pray for him, and even asked her to call if she could.

Within four hours of sending that email, I received a phone call from her. She said, "Hi, this is Joan Hunter." At the "Hi, this is…" I already knew who it was. She didn't even have to tell me her name because I had heard that voice from the videos so many times. I was amazed. It was a holiday and she is a very busy lady and she took time to call us! Little did I know at the time but when she received that email the Lord spoke to her. "This one is yours," He said to her, "You are going to have to walk him through his healing." She has since told us that this kind of thing only happens rarely to her and she normally lets her ministry team make the first calls. I ran into the bedroom and said, "Joe, Joan Hunter is on the phone," and handed the handset to him.

JOE

Joan, like she almost always does, asked me about my condition. She then proceeded to pray over my body and tell the pain to leave, my vertebrae to align, inflammation to go, nerves to be restored, and my body to line up with the Word of God, all in the name of Jesus. "How do you feel now?" she asked. "I don't feel any different," I said disappointedly. She said, "Hmm." Then she proceeded to pray again saying very much the same thing. "How do you feel now?" she asked again. "No different," I said again, this time almost in tears. "Hmm, you should be healed," she said with conviction, "I am going to go back to the Lord on this one," she said in a perplexed voice. "In the meantime I want you to go to a church that really believes in healing," she continued, "There is a church in Concord near you by the name of Impact Church. It is pastored by a lady named Donna Wise and her husband Terry. I ministered there a few months ago and Terry was miraculously healed of neck pain. They know the power of God and believe that He heals today. Go there and I will stay in contact with you."

Believe it or not, all I could think about at that moment was her comment that this church was led by a lady pastor. In the denomination that I grew up in, senior pastors who were female were allowed, but rare. There was still this mentality that it was fine for women to be children's pastors or music pastors, but they weren't encouraged to be the senior pastor over a church. God was already starting to break down the traditions that weren't from Him.

HEIDI

I, on the other hand, was ecstatic. Joan Hunter had called us! She felt like Joe was going to be healed! She was sending us to a church where there was hope! I couldn't wait. I had been carrying this virtually alone for so long and I needed some support from people who believed and experienced healing.

Chapter 5

HEALING BEGINS

HEIDI

I remembered where I had heard these pastors' names before. They were the ones who had brought the evangelist to North Carolina. When we went to that event, Joe had introduced himself to Pastor Terry and briefly talked to him. Many other people from Impact Church were also volunteering at the event and had been so kind and attentive to us and prayed for Joe while he was there. I looked up Impact Church on the internet and found out they even had a healing room on their campus. So they really did believe that God heals today. Joe asked me to go to the first service by myself and check it out. That opportunity came on a Wednesday night.

The moment I walked through the doors two men, who I had met at the Concord event, greeted me. "Hi," one said. "We were wondering what happened to you and your husband. We've been praying for you." I was impressed. The event was in June and here it was early October. There were so many people at that meeting and they still remembered us? Wow! I already liked this place. I don't remember much more about the service except that I liked the music, Pastor Donna, and the people I met. I just had to get Joe there, but could he tolerate it for a whole service? One of the ushers told me that they were having a prayer service that next Saturday night. That night I got Joe up, loaded him into the car, and headed off to the church. Unfortunately, that service had been canceled. Oh, Joe was devastated. "Just take me home," he said in a pitiful voice.

Joe didn't think he could sit through an entire Sunday service so we didn't go that week. Interestingly enough, at that service, a man with throat cancer was healed and also a boy who was deaf in one ear had his hearing restored. The next Saturday night they were having another service and I told Joe we needed to go.

JOE

It took a lot of encouraging, but Heidi finally convinced me that there would really be a Saturday night prayer service this time. She loaded me into the car once again and we headed off to Impact Church. We walked in and Scott, the music pastor, was singing and playing the piano. Pastor Donna was out of town, but Pastor Terry was there with many other people praying and worshiping. I hardly noticed anything else that was going on because I was so focused on the music. Pastor Scott, the keyboardist, and Justin, the drummer, were the only musicians there, but I thought I had gone to Heaven. The music was so beautiful and it seemed to fill the whole room with the Presence of the Lord. I was so dry and this felt like a gentle rain on my parched soul.

For the first time in over two years, I ignored my pain, stood, lifted my hands, closed my eyes, and got swept up in worship to my Lord. For what seemed like just moments, which actually was probably over an hour, I focused solely on Him with a true sacrifice of praise. The pain was still there, and just as intense, but the Presence of the Lord was just too strong to allow the pain to stop me. When I finally opened my eyes there were only five people remaining, Heidi and I, Scott, Justin, and Pastor Terry. We apologized for staying so long and making them feel obligated to minister to us. Scott said, "I will play as long as there is someone here who wants to worship. Don't feel bad at all. It was my pleasure." I walked over to Pastor Terry and wrapped my arms around him. He is a tall man and he towered over me. He really didn't know me and I could tell he was uncomfortable by my hug, but after the initial awkwardness, he wrapped his long arms around me and began to pray for me. I am so grateful that he did. It locked me into that church for the next seven years and formed a friendship like I had never had with a pastor before.

Over the next months we would go to Impact every time the doors were open. I only missed when the pain was so bad that I wasn't able to get into the car. Initially, I would go to the services, sit hunched over with my head in my hands trying to manage the pain, and try to wrap my head around what was being preached. The people there were wonderful and really believed God was going to heal me. They dispelled all the lies the enemy had been telling me about healing. One lady, named Lynnsey, would tell me, "You don't even have to have faith. We will have it for you. We will pick up your mat and take you to Jesus." She of course was referring to the story of the four friends who carried the lame man on his mat, tore off the roof of a house, and lowered him down through the hole to Jesus who, in turn, seeing their faith, healed the man completely in Luke 5:17-26. "You just keep coming up and getting prayed for until you are totally whole. You are going to be healed," she would tell me. We also showed up at the healing rooms every time they were open and many different people prayed for me and encouraged me to persevere for my healing.

HEIDI

The group from the healing rooms invited us to come to a healing meeting that was being hosted at a church in High Point, North Carolina. The speaker was Randy Clark, a well-known and effective healing minister. I was concerned that the trip would be too much for Joe, but I felt very strongly that we should go. After a very long and grueling trip in the rain and getting lost along the way, we arrived. Gratefully the group had saved us seats because there were hundreds in attendance and the place was packed. We listened to Randy minister about the healing power of God and how we as believers have been given the command, as well as the authority, to "heal the sick, raise the dead, cast out devils, cleanse lepers and tell the people that the Kingdom of Heaven is at hand."

After the service he called his healing teams forward and asked anyone to come up to one of the team members if they wanted healing. I took Joe and headed to the front of the sanctuary. There were people everywhere standing in lines to be prayed for. Joe was having trouble standing, so I found a line and sat him down to wait. Just then I noticed that Randy was still on the stage and he only had one person who he was talking to. I said, "Come on Joe. Let's go and get prayed for by Randy Clark." Reluctantly Joe came with me.

Randy treated us like we were the only people there. He gave us his full attention for more than 30 minutes. He listened to us intently as we described what Joe was going through. Then he prayed for him. Afterward, Randy said something to us that we will never forget:

> Don't look to the "big name" healing evangelists
> for healing. God can use anyone to heal you. There
> was a time a while back when I had back issues and
> could hardly walk. I could not put my foot down
> on the floor. I could not put any pressure on it or
> straighten my leg without excruciating pain. I ended
> up going to the doctor who found I had neurologi-
> cal damage to my spine.
>
> I went to a physical therapist for ninety days, six
> days a week. I could not walk without crutches,
> could not sit in a chair without exacerbating the
> problem, and was reduced to lying on a mat or lying
> in bed. Eventually, I was given two epidurals. The
> physical therapist told me that if they did not help,
> then I would probably need back surgery. I had
> three herniated discs and two pinched nerves, along
> with two forms of arthritis in my spine. The epidur-
> als did not help.

I went to many "big name" healing evangelists and friends who have strong healing gifts but was not healed through their prayers. Instead, I was healed through two people who are not noted for healing. My son, Josh, called me and said, "Dad, I believe God wants to heal you." Then he prayed for me. While I received partial healing at that time, my full healing only came several weeks later. An email message from a businessman in Louisiana reported that he was granted an open vision of my back, seeing the spine and the nerves going out of the spine. He also saw Jesus tell him how to pray. He acted out everything the Lord was showing him, even though he was in a church service at the time.

The next day after waking up, I discovered I was completely healed. Without knowing about that prayer, I was able to walk without crutches for the first time in ninety days, walk stairs normally, and was free from the excruciating pain I experienced when putting my left foot on the ground.

This revelation from Randy totally changed my mindset about healing. Christians have somehow left healing to the professionals. God didn't design the Church that way. If I'm a believer, then God's healing power resides in me through His Holy Spirit. No one has any more of the Holy Spirit than anyone else. There is no big Holy Spirit for adults and little Holy Spirit for children. There is only one Holy Spirit. The only difference is how much of *us* the Holy Spirit has, not how much of Him we have. Jesus' command is to all who believe and we need to start operating in His authority. Then our world will know that Jesus is the Christ.

JOE

Gradually, over the course of the next year, my healing did take place. Every time there was an invitation for people to come up for healing I would go. Every time the healing rooms were open I was there to be prayed for. Even if there was no invitation, I would ask those who I knew really believed in praying with authority to pray over me. We were there at the church every time the doors were open.

At first I had faith in the faith of others. Eventually, my own faith in God began to strengthen as my healing began to manifest. The healing would come in plateaus. I would get a breakthrough and then I would stay there for a while. The enemy would come along and say, "That's all you are going to get." I would say, "No devil, it's not. I'm going to be totally healed." Then I would proceed to command the pain in my back and legs and tell it to go in the name of Jesus. Then I would get another breakthrough and the whole process would happen again and again as I inched closer and closer to total healing.

Early on in this process I decided to stop seeing the doctors and started to wean myself off all my medications. None of them were really helping me anyway. I was so addicted to some of the drugs that it took me months of carving off little slivers of each pill to reduce the dosage enough to finally get completely off of them. As I did that, my brain began to heal and I was able to focus more. If anyone, including doctors, spoke anything negative over me, I would verbally "cut it off" in the name of Jesus. The Lord's thoughts about me are good and not evil, plans to prosper me and not to harm me, to give me a hope and a future (see Jer. 29:11). I wasn't about to let the words of men override the Word of the Lord over me.

Every time I went to Impact I would seek out Terry. He would encourage me with stories of his encounters with the Lord. He told me the story of his miraculous healing when Joan Hunter came to their church. Terry had been suffering with incredible neck pain and headaches from misaligned vertebrae in his neck that occurred when he was in a traumatic accident 16 years prior. You could literally feel the lump on the back of his neck where the vertebrae were twisted and he said his wife Donna couldn't even bear to touch it because it felt so "gross."

He was sitting in the back of the sanctuary, with pain and a headache, running the sound board while Joan was talking. All of a sudden he heard her say that there was someone there with pain in their neck that was going to be healed if they would come up to the front to be prayed for. She said she was going to break the trauma off. Terry said that if Joan would have just said neck pain, he probably wouldn't have responded, but when she mentioned trauma, he knew she was talking about him. He immediately left the sound board and made his way to the front.

"Now that's unusual," she said. "Pastors usually are reluctant to come up for prayer." "But I want to be healed," Terry said. Joan laid her hands on his neck and commanded the pain to go, inflammation to cease, and the vertebrae to line up in the name of Jesus. She also commanded the trauma from the accident to leave and not return. The pain abated somewhat and the headache was gone, but he could still feel the lump where the vertebrae were twisted. "Well, at least the pain is better," he thought.

He went home that night and awoke in the morning staring at the ceiling, not really thinking about anything in particular, and definitely not about healing. All of a sudden he felt something shifting in his neck. He was lying perfectly still and not moving his head at all. "I knew what was happening," he told me, "but I wasn't even praying or even thinking about my neck at the time." Just then his vertebrae popped into alignment, the lump was gone and there was no more pain. He didn't even tell Donna at the time, but waited until she was in the car with him on their way back to church to see Joan. "Look at my neck," he told Donna. She looked where the lump used to be and exclaimed in surprise, "Your neck is straight and the lump is gone!" And it has stayed in place ever since.

Terry told me about an event in their lives that changed the way they viewed their relationship with the Lord. They had heard there was more of God than what they were experiencing and decided to attend a conference that focused on His supernatural power. During one of the ministry times, they both went to the front of the church to be prayed for. One of the ministers laid his hands on them and prayed over them. They both felt God's supernatural Presence like they never had before. They were so overwhelmed that neither of them said a word to each other. Finally, when they got back to their car, they turned to one other and asked, "Did you feel that?" When they compared their experience, it was exactly the same. This set them on a quest to experience all God had for them so they could share it with others and become all the Lord had designed them to be.

After this encounter Donna would get prophetic pictures as God showed her what He was doing. Terry would have prophetic dreams and then wake up, open his eyes, and see what seemed to be a movie screen pulled down in front of him that finished the vision he had started in his sleep. He told me about encounters with angels and with the Lord that made me jealous for the same. At one point I wanted to start seeing God's supernatural power so badly that I asked Terry to lay hands on me and pray that the Lord would start to show me signs too. I didn't realize how quickly the Lord would answer his prayer.

Chapter 6

GOD'S UNIVERSITY

JOE

God is so faithful and so personal. I'm such a literal person and need tangible things that will keep my faith strong so that I can share them with others. Little did I know when I asked for signs that He would answer me with literal "signs." The next Sunday, after Terry prayed that the Lord would show me signs, he and Donna invited Heidi and me to go to lunch with them. I was feeling so bad and worn out that I asked Heidi if we could just go home. She reluctantly complied, but she really needed to fellowship with other people.

While we were on our way to our house I realized her need to socialize and told her that I would stick it out and we should go to the restaurant. That caused her to drive to the place a different way than if we had traveled straight from our church. We passed by a large church on the way and a car pulled out in front of us. The license plate on the car was "JHVRAPHA." When I saw it, I stopped talking, turned to Heidi in amazement, and said, "Do you see that plate? God is talking to us through that license plate. He is saying, 'I am Jehovah Rapha, the Lord who heals you!'" We were stunned. When we got to the restaurant that was all we could talk about. The Lord was confirming that He was going to heal me.

The next week Heidi was traveling in Matthews, which is a town adjacent to Charlotte. She had to stop for a red light and she thought she recognized the truck in front of her. She soon realized it was the wrong color vehicle, but when she looked at the license plate it encouraged her greatly. It read "HEALD!" She couldn't wait to come home and share the news. God was again confirming His intent to heal by showing her a license plate that she interpreted as healed!

The next day I was setting up an account for Heidi on PayPal. Before I could set up the account, the website required me to type in a series of characters from a picture at the bottom of the screen so that the site knows that I'm a real person and not a computer. Normally it's a combination of letters and numbers or a common word. This was not. The characters I was instructed to type were "JHHVH." It reminded me of the Jewish abbreviation for the name Jehovah. Just to make sure this wasn't a coincidence, I tried it again. It was completely different. I figured out the chances that something like this could happen and calculated that it was one chance in over a billion-billion. I interpreted these three signs as the Lord saying, "I am Jehovah Rapha, the Lord who heals you. You are going to be healed for I am Jehovah." I would repeat this prophecy over and over to myself many times a day through the course of my healing.

License plates, electronic signs, street signs, emails, texts, and other kinds of written things started appearing on a frequent basis. We never looked for them; they just kind of showed up when we needed them. Some would come to encourage us. Others showed us how God wanted us to invest some of our money. At times they would come as a direct answer to our prayers or confirmation of what God was saying through His Word or through His messengers.

Donna Wise is a very gifted pastor and teacher. She is the most gifted, in my opinion, on the topic of what some call "inner healing." She and Terry own several successful professional counseling centers in North Carolina and use many of these biblical principles with their clients when they are allowed to. Very early in our time at Impact Church we were privileged to attend one of the extended seminars they used to have. I had taught "young married" Sunday school for about ten years and had helped many couples find their way to a healthier and a happier future. Many of the subjects she taught I had also taught, but the insights the Lord had given her were far beyond what I conveyed in my classes.

It wasn't surprising to learn that many Christians may put on a good front in public, but in private they are totally different. What was surprising was the depth of the dysfunction. Anger, bitterness, unforgiveness, depression, loneliness, sadness, self-doubt, and criticism are constant companions of so many in the Church. They live inside cages of their own making and doubt that God even cares about them. Most had help getting there because of some form of abuse in their lives from parents, siblings, or other family members. Later on others joined in the fray. Spouses, pastors, teachers, employers, and even so-called friends helped them in the making of their personal prisons. Whether the abuse was actual or perceived, physical, mental, emotional, or sexual, the bars become stronger and more plentiful. For so many there seems to be no way out.

Donna has one statement that I feel sums up how Christians can gain their freedom. "But God...." The two words appear in various forms hundreds of times in Scripture. For every excuse of why a person feels they should stay in their cage, this is the rebuttal. "I don't know how I can ever forgive my parents." "But God...." I don't know how to get out of this depression." "But God...." I don't know how to stop this critical spirit I have." "But God...."

The first class of the seminar was always a revelation of how our heavenly Father sees all of us. Each one of His children is God's masterpiece. Each one of us is as important to Him as His other sons and daughters. He is no respecter of persons. We are all His favorites. We are children of God our Father, who gave everything He had in the person of His only begotten Son, Jesus the Messiah, who saved (sozo) us and set us free. He even made us joint heirs with Jesus (see Rom. 8:17). He has given all of us what we need for life and godliness (see 2 Pet. 1:3). Each of us is that important to God and each of us has a God planned destiny waiting to be discovered and walked in. It is the devil who comes to steal, kill, and destroy—not God. Jesus came to give us life and give it to us more abundantly (see John 10:10).

The rest of the seminar was filled with teaching that exposed the toxic lies of the enemy that are contrary to this truth. They opened the eyes of the participants to their own wrong thoughts that were keeping them imprisoned. There were many group sessions with hands-on exercises that brought out each person's particular issues and helped them to find practical answers to overcome them. Heidi and I were so impressed that we volunteered to be facilitators at most of those seminars from then on. We saw so many people delivered and their lives changed over those years and we are so grateful for that opportunity to learn to help others in that area of ministry.

HEIDI

A significant thing happened during one of the inner healing seminars where we helped out as facilitators. We often wondered why the Lord said that through Joe's progressive miracle he would learn how to not "lose" his healing and to stay healthy. We had seen many people get miraculously healed, but there were a few who would get the same thing back again or even something worse. The Lord was about to show us at least one reason why this happens.

In one of the seminar's breakout sessions, Joe and I had a group of all women. One of the questions that each person had to answer was, "What do you think is keeping you from your God-given destiny?" After each one wrote their answer on a piece of paper, Joe asked if anyone was willing to share their answer. In a split second, one woman, we will call her Dana (not her real name), said boldly, "Oh I will." She then proceeded to say that she had been suffering for years with debilitating fibromyalgia and arthritis. She had applied for Social Security disability, but that was still in process. She could hardly get up in the morning to take her kids to school and even housework was almost impossible. She was the sister of one of the ladies in the church and the two of them wanted to start a small business together, but because of her illness she couldn't do what she felt destined to do.

Dana's husband, her sister, and her sister's husband had come to the seminar also, but were in other groups. Joe said, "Well then, let's just pray right now so you can be healed and get that thing out of the way. Ladies, would you please lay your hands on her and agree with me while I pray." He prayed just like we had been taught. "In the name of Jesus, I command you fibromyalgia, go right now! Arthritis, go! All inflammation and pain go! Muscles be restored. Joints go back to normal and cartilage and bone be restored in the name of Jesus."

Because his faith wasn't quite mature yet, he hedged, "Now Dana, sometimes there are instantaneous miracles and sometimes there are progressive..." He didn't even get the word "healings" out of his mouth before she started shouting, "I'm healed, I'm healed, I'm healed!" The shock on Joe's face was priceless. God had at least confirmed one principle we had learned. It's not about how much faith we have; it's about obedience. We are responsible for the natural and the Lord is responsible for the supernatural. She ran out of the room to find her husband, sister, and brother-in-law. They couldn't believe it. She was totally restored. She bent and twisted and raised her hands above her head. She jumped and shouted and let everyone know she was healed.

JOE

For the next three months, every time I would see Dana or her sister I would ask how she was doing. And for three months the report came back that she was still enjoying her healing. She was driving her children to school, doing housework and even stood on a table to clean the ceiling fan. Then one day her sister told me it all came back. "Really, the fibromyalgia and the arthritis both came back?" I asked, "What happened?" "Well you remember when she told you that she had applied for disability? If she had no pain she couldn't qualify for the disability check and she wanted that more," she said. I was floored. I couldn't believe it. I had been on disability and gladly gave up my pain even knowing I would lose that income.

As Jesus told His disciples:

> *When an unclean spirit goes out of a man, he goes through dry places, seeking rest, and finds none. Then he says, "I will return to my house from which I came." And when he comes, he finds it empty, swept, and put in order. Then he goes and takes with him seven other spirits more wicked than himself, and they enter and dwell there; and the last state of that man is worse than the first. So shall it also be with this wicked generation* (Matthew 12:43-45).

Remember, if we don't fill that empty place that is vacated when we are healed with a mindset from the Spirit of God, then that place gets filled back up with the same toxic lies of the enemy that got us into our situation in the first place. It opens the door for the problem to come back in even a greater measure than before. We must be ever vigilant to maintain our healing by being self-lessly obedient to His Word and His plan for our lives.

Chapter 7

BACK TO WORK

JOE

It had been a wonderful year. My pain continued to abate and my mind was healing also. I was ready to go back to work. When I started on disability, the counselor told us that over 90 percent of the people who get on Social Security disability never get off. Praise God I wasn't going to be one of those. Graciously the president of the computer software company where I was an analyst said that he would give me my old job back. This was definitely an answer to prayer and a blessing from the Lord. Not many places will take a chance on someone who has been disabled for that long.

It was good for my brain to have to be stretched again. The medications and stress had caused it to have many memory "holes." I remember one time I was trying to think of the name of my uncle, the oldest of my mother's three brothers. I had grown up knowing all of their names even as a small child. Tom, Dave, and...? I couldn't remember no matter how hard I tried. Finally I asked Heidi what his name was. "John," she said. "Oh yes. Tom, Dave, and John. Wow I can't believe that was missing," I replied with a sigh. This was one "fact" among many that seemed to be behind walls in my mind. Once I was able to pull the walls down and re-establish those facts, I could remember them again. To this day I'm still excavating old memories and putting them in their proper place.

HEIDI

As Joe was being healed, I was also regaining my freedom. It was no longer necessary for me to be on call every hour of every day for him. I could finally have my own schedule and it was wonderful. One day Joe and I were driving somewhere in the car and we were having a discussion. Suddenly there was an uncomfortable chill in the conversation. "I feel like a wall just went up between us," he said. I felt it too, but I didn't know why it happened. As I began to think about it, the reason came to the forefront of my mind. "I guess I'm angry with you for being sick for all those years and keeping me a virtual prisoner in my own home," I said. I hadn't thought about it until that very moment, but I realized those years had taken a severe toll on me also and I resented him for that. I needed healing as much as he did. It just was more emotional and mental than physical. With the help of the Holy Spirit I have been able to get that restoration. We must always remember that many times sickness and disease affect more than just one person. We need to be aware that caregivers and other family members may also need healing and minister to them as well.

JOE

It was by going back to work that God reinforced two important principles in my life. One had to do with the word He spoke to Heidi about staying healthy. I had lost, over my working history, about five and a half years of working income. Three of those years were due to my disability. Retirement age was on the horizon and I felt that I hadn't done a good job of investing for the future. I was determined to make up for that now. Not only did I work at the software company during the day, I also worked for another computer company during my off-hours. Sometimes I would work 80 to 90 hours a week total. Not that working that many hours is wrong, but my reliance on myself to assure our financial future was. As I have said before, too many people, once they are healed, go right back into things that got them there in the first place. In my case, the Lord had always taken care of us financially. Why was I thinking He wouldn't do that for us in the future? When the Lord showed me that I was working those extra hours out of fear and not obedience, I had to repent. "Lord," I prayed, "I trust You. You love me and You have always provided. I will not work ever again out of fear, but will always remember that You hold my future in Your hands." Now I work for one company and work a normal number of hours per week doing a job that I enjoy. I no longer fear for the future because I know the One who is faithful.

The second principle that God reinforced was how much He loves every one of us. One day, about a year after returning to work, I was feeling a little down and just needed some comfort from the Lord. I asked God, very innocently but very sincerely, to let me know that He loved me in some tangible way. As I said in the previous chapter, the Lord often talks to me in signs. But this day I wasn't really thinking along those lines. I just wanted the Lord to let me know He loved me in an undeniable way. Of course we have the Scriptures that let us know that, but I wanted something a little more personal.

That very afternoon, not more than four hours after that prayer, while I was leaving a store parking lot, an SUV happened to catch my eye. It had been parked about five cars down from my van. There was something strange about the license plate. You see, in North Carolina, most plates are three letters, a dash, and then four numbers. This plate was eight letters with no spaces. As I looked, tears came to my eyes and a tremendous warm feeling of God's love flowed like warm honey over my entire being. Even as I'm writing this, that feeling is overwhelming me again. The plate had the embossed letters, "ILUVUJOE" emblazoned on it. I just had to stop my van, pull out my cell phone and take a picture. I thought, "Just think how much God has to love me to take the only car in North Carolina with that plate, put it in this parking lot, on this day, at this time, and get me here so I can see that God, the ruler of the universe, loves me. Not only does He love the world, He loves me!"

At that moment I heard the Holy Spirit speak to my heart and say that this event wasn't only to let me know that He loves me individually and personally as His child, but He wanted me to tell this story to those I come in contact with and let them know that He loves them the same way.

Since that time, I have told this story to many people and have seen the effect it has had on their lives. Most people can't believe it until I pull out my cell phone and show them the picture, but the response is almost always the same—their eyes begin to water as they start to understand the love the Father has for them. Not just "God so loves the world" in general, but the Father loves them and knows them by name.

Some people have asked me if I'm someone special that God would do this for me. I tell them that I'm just as special as any other child of God, but I did one thing that most of His children don't do. I asked. I believe if someone will dare to ask, the Father will answer them also. Maybe not in a license plate, but in a way that is very unique and special to them.

I shared this story just recently with Tabitha, a young woman we know from church. You could just see the countenance on her face change when she read the words on the license plate, "ILUVUJOE." I told her that if she would ask the Father, He would show His love to her in her own special way. She asked, and the Lord answered. This girl had grown up in difficult circumstances and had a very strained relationship with her own father. One night, the same week, she had a dream. She was having a picture taken with her father. Just before the flash of the camera, her father leaned over and wrapped his arms around her in a warm parental embrace. She was surprised and overwhelmed by the love she felt at that moment. She couldn't resist that love even if she wanted to.

When she woke up the Lord revealed that her earthly father in the dream was symbolic of her heavenly Father, and it was really Him embracing her and showing her how much He loves her! It was her "ILUVUTABITHA" moment and the Lord expressed it in the way it would make the most impact on her. When Tabitha told us the story, you could see the glow on her face because she knew how much her heavenly Father loves her!

Through my "ILUVUJOE" encounter with God, I believe I have learned something else about His love for us. God is an infinite God. Now I was taught that infinity divided by anything is always still infinity. Therefore, infinity divided by the number of humans born since the time of creation (over 100 billion) is still infinity. So the Father, who is infinite love, loves you infinitely. Because He loves you infinitely, you truly can say He loves you best. You are His favorite. You can truthfully say that you are His favorite without taking anything away from anyone else. All of His infinite nature is at your disposal. He has infinite time, resources, mercy, grace, and patience because of His infinite love for you. We all are His favorites and He is the only One who can do that because He is infinitely powerful, infinitely just, and infinitely good.

The Lord showed this to me in a practical way when Heidi and I went to the beach with our granddaughters. We had built a large sand castle with a moat. The girls were going down to the shore with buckets, scooping up the water and running back to fill up the moat over and over again. Did I tell them to stop doing that because the ocean would run out of water and there wouldn't be anything left for me? Of course I didn't. We could line every person on the earth up on the seashore and they could scoop buckets of water out of the ocean as fast as they possibly could and the ocean level wouldn't even perceptively drop at all. That is the love of the Father. There is more than enough for anyone and everyone. And there is certainly more than enough for you.

There is an old song that they used to sing in the church I grew up in:

> It is no secret,
>
> what God can do.
>
> What He's done for others,
>
> He'll do for *you*.

I challenge you to ask the Father today to show you how much He loves *you*. Ask Him to show this to you in a way that will impact you enough that you won't forget it even in the hardest times of your life. He is faithful, able, and willing to show His children how much He loves them and that every one of us is His favorite.

In fact, why don't you ask Him to do that right now? Then, write the date on the line provided below or on your calendar.

I asked the Father to show me how much He loves me on:

*Date:*_____

When the Father answers your request, please email us at info@encouragingpeople.com and let us know, but don't stop asking until He does. He delights in showing you His love in ways you alone can fully understand. Sometimes He is just waiting to set the stage for some amazing way to show you when you need it most.

> *How precious it is, Lord, to realize that you are thinking about me constantly! I can't even count how many times a day your thoughts turn toward me. And when I waken in the morning, you are still thinking of me!* (Psalm 139:17-18 TLB)

Chapter 8

TRAINING IN THE MIRACULOUS

JOE

We want to relate some testimonies of the miraculous power of God. Each one, whether we were directly involved or not, taught us more about the authority we have as believers in Christ over all the power of the enemy. Every one of us should bless and not curse (see Rom. 12:14). Every one of us should be going around doing good and healing all who are under the power of the devil (see Acts 10:38 NIV).

One night the men from Impact Church were invited to a special men's meeting at another church. There were men there from several other churches in the area. We had a great time of eating, worshiping, and teaching that night as the men joined together in unity of purpose. After the speaker was done teaching, he asked if there were any men there who needed prayer for anything. Several men raised their hands. Then he asked the other men in attendance to pick a person, ask what they were in need of, and pray in faith believing that what we asked for would be accomplished. Pastor Terry and I picked the same man and asked him what he wanted prayer for. He told us that he was deaf in one ear and wanted his hearing back. I had never prayed for a deaf person who was healed so I looked to Pastor Terry for guidance. He laid hands on the man's ears, I laid my hands on the man's feet, and the other men laid their hands on him too. Terry began to pray that the man's deaf ear would be healed and for his hearing to return in the authority of Jesus. When we were finished praying, much to our surprise, the man said he could hear out of his ear again.

Little did we know how much of a miracle this was. The man went on to tell us that the reason he had been deaf in his ear was because he had a tumor wrapped around the bones of that middle ear that facilitate hearing. When they removed the tumor during the surgery, they had to take out the bones too. There was no way he should be hearing this well. Wow! God hadn't only restored his hearing, but had done a creative miracle to accomplish it.

A few weeks later we heard more of the story. The man had gone home and when he walked down the hallway he heard a noise. He asked his wife, "What is that noise I'm hearing?" "That's the bathroom fan," she said. After that he walked to the other end of the house and told his wife to say something so he could see if he could hear her. She didn't shout, but said something to him in a normal voice, and he could hear her perfectly from that distance without a problem. Yay, God!

I had always wondered what happened to that man. Was he still healed? Two years after that, Terry and I were at an outdoor worship event in the center of the city of Concord, North Carolina. They had a number of worship bands and special speakers there. A man walked up to the microphone and started to share a testimony of how God had healed his deaf ear. We recognized the testimony and the man. He was still healed, still rejoicing, and still sharing his testimony. Praise the Lord.

HEIDI

During this time period, we got an email from Joan. "You need to go on this church website and watch this video," she said. The video was of a woman who was attending one of Joan's healing school services. This lady had arachnoiditis, the same disease that Joe suffered from, for 13 years. She described the pain this way: "It's like sliding down a razor blade into iodine." She had been prayed for by many healing evangelists, but to no avail, and had almost given up.

When she heard about Joan, she told the Lord, "All the people who have prayed for me in the past didn't even understand what I'm going through. If this lady can tell me, I know You will heal me." Joan was calling out people who needed healing in their back and this woman came up for prayer. After many people were healed, Joan turned to this woman. "What do you need prayer for?" she asked. "I have excruciating pain in my lower spine. The nerves are matted together and..." the woman began saying. But before she could continue Joan said, "And you have..." and began to describe all of her symptoms entirely. The lady was amazed. "How did you know?" she asked. "There is a man named Joe in North Carolina who was completely healed of this very same thing and you can be healed too," Joan replied. As soon as Joan prayed, the symptoms disappeared in a moment and she went back to her church dancing and rejoicing. Her pastor was so amazed at the difference in her that he wanted to know what had happened. She was able to tell him of God's goodness and healing power. She also came back to the meeting the next night and gave her testimony.

When Joan Hunter would come to North Carolina, we would try to go to her meetings and healing schools. Joan's mission statement, "Taking the healing power of God beyond the four walls of the church to the four corners of the earth," should be the mission of every believer, and we were hungry to learn everything we could about healing people physically, mentally, emotionally, spiritually, and financially. Every time we went, we were amazed at how many people got healed in each meeting. During the schools, she taught how to pray for people through practical examples. For every area of need, she would ask people to come up to the front and begin to instruct us on how to pray for that issue. Most of the time, the person would be healed or have the need met right away. Then she would have the students use that knowledge to pray for others in the class and many times we would see the same results.

Sometimes Joan would come to Charlotte to do a taping of Sid Roth's TV show *It's Supernatural!* She is one of his favorites and has been on his show more times than any other guest. We would make sure we were there to chauffeur her around, if she needed it, and attend the taping of the shows. Several times she had Joe give his testimony and help her while she prayed for the sick. After the show was done, she would stay around and pray for the studio audience and backstage personnel.

Sometimes there were so many in need of healing she would recruit us to come and pray for people too. We started to see people we prayed for there being healed right in front of our eyes. We found that there was just as much need for emotional and mental healing as there was for physical healing. We were learning to become bolder, because we were seeing the power of God change people's lives when we prayed with the authority Jesus had given to us through His name.

JOE

I was getting so excited about all the healings we were seeing, but I wanted to see more. In my exuberance I told the Lord, "I want to see all of the people we pray for healed!" Right at that moment the story in Acts about the lame man at the Gate Beautiful who was healed by Peter and John came to my mind. Jesus must have passed by that man hundreds of times. Acts 3:2 says that he was laid at the gate daily since he was born. But Jesus didn't even reach out a hand to heal him. He had the ability to heal him, but it wasn't the Father's timing. That man was to be healed later by Peter and John for a specific Kingdom purpose. (Read Acts 3 for the incredible outcome.)

I believe the Lord was teaching me that I wouldn't see all of the people I pray for healed until I was able to hear Him like Jesus did while He was on the earth. Jesus healed all of the people who came to Him, and all of the people the Father sent Him to. But God didn't direct Him to heal every person He came in contact with in every situation. I was humbled. The answer always comes back to obedience and hearing the voice of the Lord through a current and close relationship with Him.

This encounter also helped me with a challenge that I have heard people make and I didn't have an answer for. "Why," they say, "if these people who heal by faith are real, don't they go into all the hospitals and clean them out?" I believe I now know the answer. First of all, I know most of us don't hear the Father like Jesus did. Second, even if we did, I believe the Lord wouldn't tell us to do something like that except in very special situations under the direction of the Holy Spirit. For example, I have heard some testimonies of missionaries overseas going into a hospital or clinic and healing everyone there and it having a profound effect on a city or a village. It served a greater Kingdom purpose.

Let's look at what Jesus did in a similar situation:

> *After this there was a feast of the Jews, and Jesus went up to Jerusalem. Now there is in Jerusalem by the Sheep Gate a pool, which is called in Hebrew, Bethesda, having five porches. In these lay a great multitude of sick people, blind, lame, paralyzed, waiting for the moving of the water. For an angel went down at a certain time into the pool and stirred up the water; then whoever stepped in first, after the stirring of the water, was made well of whatever disease he had. Now a certain man was there who had an infirmity thirty-eight years. When Jesus saw*

*him lying there, and knew that he already had been
in that condition a long time, He said to him, "Do
you want to be made well?"*

*The sick man answered Him, "Sir, I have no man to
put me into the pool when the water is stirred up; but
while I am coming, another steps down before me."
Jesus said to him, "Rise, take up your bed and walk"
and immediately the man was made well, took up his
bed, and walked* (John 5:1-9).

Do you see it? This was probably the closest thing to a hospital
in Jesus' day. It was like an emergency room. Here all the "patients"
were lying around waiting to be treated. When the angel came
down at a certain time and stirred the water, the first person who
was able to get into the pool was healed. The rest had to just wait
for the next opportunity. Jesus walked into the midst of that "hospital" and picked one man to heal him. I'm assuming there were
dozens or possibly over a hundred people there. Why only that *one*?
It certainly wasn't because he was more righteous or more deserv-
ing than the rest, because later Jesus warned him to *"Sin no more,
lest a worse thing come upon you."* It was because that man was the
one the Father told Jesus to heal at that time for His own purposes.
Read the rest of the story to see the outcome.

I don't want to suggest that we should just sit around twiddling
our thumbs and wait for the Lord to give us somebody's name. We
have done that for too long and used it as an excuse for not praying for people. We need to have the compassion of Jesus for people
out there in our world and be available to pray for anyone. Then
we need to ask the Lord every day to identify those He wants us

to pray for. We should always be ready for Him to show His glory through us.

> *And when Jesus went out He saw a great multitude;*
> *and He was moved with compassion for them, and*
> *healed their sick* (Matthew 14:14).

So now our prayer is that someday we can see every person who comes to us, and every person He identifies or sends us to, healed. We want to be so close to the Lord that we can feel His heartbeat and hear His voice clearly. To re-present Him well.

So why did I write "re-present?" That isn't a typo. In the past, most, including me, haven't done a good job of presenting the Lord to people as He really is. Because of that, the world has a negative and improper image of our God. I'm now determined to take what I have learned about Him and present Him all over again to all those I meet, as He really is. I want to "re-present" Him, so they can really know this wonderful, loving God whom we serve as His beloved children.

I want to note that when it comes to preaching the Gospel, we don't need to wait for the Holy Spirit to point them out. Jesus preached the Good News of the Kingdom to everyone and told us to do the same.

> *And He said to them, "Go into all the world and*
> *preach the gospel to every creature"* (Mark 16:15).

So you don't have to ask what God's will is when it comes to evangelism. This verse is quite clear about what His will is.

I want to note here that I struggled whether to put this part about healing into this book. I didn't want to misrepresent what we can ask God for concerning His healing power in our lives today. The Lord gave me peace about it, so I left it in. A few months later, I was watching Bill Johnson being interviewed by Sid Roth on *It's Supernatural!* about God's goodness.

> Sid: "What did Jesus model about healing?"
>
> Bill: "Just in general. He healed everyone who came to him, number one, and He healed everyone the Father sent Him to. He didn't heal everyone who was sick who was alive, because we know He healed the one man at the pool of Bethesda, and there were many others around the pool. Tragically our theology today tends to be built around what didn't happen, instead of what God did do. But Jesus healed everyone that came to Him and everyone the Father directed Him to. That is the only standard I'm willing to follow."

My mouth nearly dropped to the floor and I got so excited. The words that Bill spoke, and the example that he used, were just what the Lord had told me. It was a confirmation to me that what I had written was the truth.

We started to minister as much outside the church as we did inside. One of my friends was having troubles financially. His wife's job provided the primary income and he stayed home to school his children. When he could, he would do handyman work, but that was sporadic at best. They needed him to be earning more income to make ends meet. I met with him and we discussed this problem. We agreed that God wanted to meet his family's financial needs and that the Lord was fully capable of finding jobs for him to do. I asked Him to trust God and pray that the Lord would bring the jobs.

From that point on, every time I saw him I would say, "Be blessed and highly favored" and "You are God's favorite." I prayed that God would show him His goodness and faithfulness. Within a month or two he had so much business he had to find other people to help him. He did work on the home of a man whose business manages hundreds of rental properties. That man was so impressed with the speed and quality of the work that he told him that he could keep him busy for as many hours a week as he wanted fixing his rentals. He also said he could have his pick of the jobs. Thank You, Jesus!

Jesus said, "Assuredly, I say to you, whatever you bind on earth will be bound in heaven, and whatever you loose on earth will be loosed in heaven" (Matt. 18:18).

We were learning that we are our heavenly Father's children. We have the power to bless or curse. Sometimes cursing comes in the form of speaking negative things over our own lives or the lives of others. We need to choose to bless. We need to speak not what we see, but what we want to see, and make sure that it lines up with the Word of God. The Lord lets the rain fall on both the just and the unjust. We want and need to be more like Jesus in everything we say and do.

Chapter 9

D. E. A. R.

JOE

A blueprint isn't just a picture of the thing that is to be built. It's a plan that not only has different types of drawings of that thing but has detailed instructions on how to build it. In terms of a house, which Jesus used as an illustration for our lives, the blueprint also contains specifications, materials, measurements, placement, and directions to help the builder construct that house correctly. At first glance, by those who have little experience, blueprints can be confusing and hard to read. This is why most builders apprentice under an experienced builder to find out how to turn a blueprint into what the architect had envisioned in his mind when he drew it.

God is our Architect and the blueprint for our lives is His Word. It contains everything we need to achieve our God-given destiny, which is to look like Jesus. But, for many people, it is hard to read and understand how to turn those words into reality in their own situations. This is why the Lord created discipleship, so we could be apprentices under someone who knows how to read the blueprint and help us to implement it into our own lives.

One night I had a dream. In my dream four large letters were standing on top of each other. The letters spelled DEAR. I knew that the letters stood for something and so I asked the Lord what that was. He said, "The D stands for demonstrate and the A stands for activate." Then I woke up. After I was fully awake I asked the Lord what the other letters stood for. He said, "Get up and get a piece of paper and something to write with and I will tell you." I jumped up and did just what He said. He told me the other letters stand for equip and release. He said, "This is how Jesus taught and this is how I desire My children to be taught."

Demonstrate

Equip

Activate

Release

Here is what I have found as I have sought the Lord on the D.E.A.R. process:

Demonstrate

> *That which was from the beginning, which we have heard, which we have seen with our eyes, which we have looked upon, and our hands have handled, concerning the Word of life—the life was manifested, and we have seen, and bear witness, and declare to you that eternal life which was with the Father and was manifested to us—that which we have seen and heard we declare to you, that you also may have fellowship with us; and truly our fellowship is with the Father and with His Son Jesus Christ. And these things we write to you that your joy may be full* (1 John 1:1-4).

Jesus demonstrated what He preached to His disciples. When He commanded that they go and heal the sick, He showed them how to heal every kind of sickness and disease. When He said raise the dead, they observed Him raise the dead right before their eyes. When He said cast out devils, they saw Him not only cast out one but a legion of demons. When He said cleanse the lepers, He would show them how to cleanse one or even ten at a time. He said, "When you do these works, tell the people the Kingdom of Heaven is already here." Then He preached that very message to the multitudes so His disciples could see how. When they didn't understand what He was saying, He took them aside and explained it in terms that they could understand. The way Jesus taught was "hands on." He could really instruct, "Do what I say *and* what I do."

I have seen pastors and other leaders in the church teach the principles of the Kingdom but not actively demonstrate, to those who are under their care, how to live them out in their everyday lives. They preach healing, but they never demonstrate healing. They tell people to witness, but aren't witnessing themselves outside the church. Some don't do it out of fear of failure, but others because they haven't truly learned how themselves. Their people go out and try, but they too flounder and many fail because they have no mentor to show them how.

So they feel guilty because they don't see success and eventually just come to the conclusion that the supernatural power of God either isn't for today or, if it is, it must be for the select few, the "professional ministers." And the work of true ministry by the children of God never gets to the people who need it the most.

The Lord was teaching me that demonstration must always be the first step in making disciples. If we can't teach people how to do something by showing it to them by example, then we need to learn how to do it. We may need to find our own mentor to disciple us. Or, if there isn't one available, the Lord will disciple us by the Holy Spirit alone as He did with Paul. We need to demonstrate how to heal the sick, raise the dead, cast out devils, cleanse lepers, and preach the Kingdom of Heaven is already here.

This is one of the reasons Jesus came to earth and chose to have disciples. He needed to demonstrate the Kingdom to them so they could live as true sons and daughters of God. And those disciples had their disciples, who had their disciples, and so on. I believe the apostle Paul said it best:

Imitate me, just as I also imitate Christ (1 Corinthians 11:1).

Equip

And He Himself gave some to be apostles, some prophets, some evangelists, and some pastors and teachers, for the equipping of the saints for the work of ministry, for the edifying of the body of Christ (Ephesians 4:11-12).

Some leaders and teachers use this verse in Ephesians as an excuse for why they aren't out there doing the work of ministry themselves. They believe that their job is just to equip. "We are just responsible to teach it, but the people are responsible for doing it, because they are the ones who are out there," is a declaration they use to make themselves feel better. Well, if you look at the rest of these verses you will see why God calls leaders who are mature in faith and in their demonstration of the Kingdom of God.

Why is it that he gives us these special abilities to do certain things best? It is that God's people will be equipped to do better work for him, building up the Church, the body of Christ, to a position of strength and maturity; until finally we all believe alike about our salvation and about our Savior, God's Son, and all become full-grown in the Lord—yes, to the point of being filled full with Christ.

Then we will no longer be like children, forever changing our minds about what we believe because someone has told us something different or has cleverly lied to us and made the lie sound like the truth. Instead, we will lovingly follow the truth at all times—speaking truly, dealing truly, living truly—and so become more and more in every way like Christ who is the Head of his body, the Church. Under his direction, the whole body is fitted together perfectly, and each part in its own special way helps the other parts, so that the whole body is healthy and growing and full of love (Ephesians 4:12-16 TLB).

In a nutshell, the Lord wants those mentors who are good examples to equip His children. These are people who are actively demonstrating the Kingdom of God in their area of ministry so they can equip the saints to do the same and keep them from going off track by speaking truth and dispelling the lies of the enemy.

The apostle James puts it this way:

But someone will say, "You have faith, and I have works." Show me your faith without your works, and I will show you my faith by my works (James 2:18).

Equipping is broken into four other "Es": *exhort, educate, empower,* and *encourage.*

Exhort

To exhort can mean "to call near." When we exhort, we call people to examine spiritual principles more closely to help them lead a mature, healthier, and more productive life in Christ. Many people believe that the commands of Jesus apply to their leaders or someone else who is "more qualified" but not to them. Part of the job of making disciples is to wake them up. This means calling them to re-examine the commands of Christ in light of the fact that they are qualified just because they are children of God alone, and to let them know these really are commands and not just suggestions.

Exhortation requires that we get into the lives of people and try to understand why they are falling short of their God-given destiny. We need to be able to get insight from the Holy Spirit as to how and where the lies of the enemy have taken root and the truth of the Word it will take to cause them to repent (change their way of thinking).

The word exhort is translated in various versions of the Bible as plead, appeal, beseech, or urge. A good example of this is when Paul, writing to the Corinthians, says:

> *Now I plead with you, brethren, by the name of our Lord Jesus Christ, that you all speak the same thing, and that there be no divisions among you, but that you be perfectly joined together in the same mind and in the same judgment* (1 Corinthians 1:10).

And in Romans 12:1 Paul says:

> *I beseech you therefore, brethren, by the mercies of God, that you present your bodies a living sacrifice, holy, acceptable to God, which is your reasonable service* (Romans 12:1).

When we exhort, it shouldn't come across as though we are their judge. There is only One Judge and that is Jesus (see John 5:22). They shouldn't feel that we are disappointed in them or that we feel superior to them. Our attitude should be like this:

> *Dear brothers and sisters, if another believer is overcome by some sin, you who are godly should gently*

and humbly help that person back onto the right path. And be careful not to fall into the same temptation yourself (Galatians 6:1 NLT).

As the Holy Spirit gives us insight to where someone is missing the mark, we should always humbly appeal to their spirit to listen to the Holy Spirit within them. He is the One who will guide them to the truth.

Educate

Much of the ministry of Jesus was teaching the principles of the Kingdom of God. Many times He used parables (stories) as examples of these precepts.

And the disciples came and said to Him, "Why do You speak to them in parables?" He answered and said to them, "Because it has been given to you to know the mysteries of the kingdom of heaven, but to them it has not been given" (Matthew 13:10-11).

Jesus was always eager to explain when the disciples didn't understand. He also built upon each principle with deeper knowledge as they were able to grasp the simpler concepts. Jesus also knew that some things could only be taught by the Holy Spirit after He went back to Heaven.

These things I have spoken to you while being present with you. But the Helper, the Holy Spirit, whom the Father will send in My name, He will teach you all things, and bring to your remembrance all things that I said to you (John 14:25-26).

There was one recorded instance where the concepts were so hard to grasp that all but His closest disciples left Him. Only the ones who realized His teaching was central to their lives remained.

> *From that time many of His disciples went back and walked with Him no more. Then Jesus said to the twelve, "Do you also want to go away?" But Simon Peter answered Him, "Lord, to whom shall we go? You have the words of eternal life"* (John 6:66-68).

Many of these principles have been lost to the church today. People have let their experiences become their theology. If something supernatural doesn't happen when they try to apply one of the principles, they conclude that it doesn't work at all. We need to teach the things that Jesus taught as a foundation. We must teach people that they need to be avid students of the Word of God. The Word does not return void. In other words it always does something. We need to keep believing and applying the Word until we see it work and teach others to do the same. Every time we don't see results, we need to be like the disciples who weren't afraid to ask Jesus why.

> *Then the disciples came to Jesus privately and said, "Why could we not cast it out?" So Jesus said to them, "Because of your unbelief; for assuredly, I say to you, if you have faith as a mustard seed, you will say to this mountain, 'Move from here to there,' and it will move; and nothing will be impossible for you"* (Matthew 17:19-20).

The Lord isn't bothered by our questions. In fact, He loves it when we come to Him for wisdom.

If you need wisdom, ask our generous God, and he will give it to you. He will not rebuke you for asking (James 1:5 NLT).

As we teach people to always pray and seek His truth, we can assure them that He will be faithful to give the answers.

Call to Me, and I will answer you, and show you great and mighty things, which you do not know (Jeremiah 33:3).

Empower

Not only do we need to exhort and educate people, we need to make sure they have the power to get the job done. We cannot do anything without the Presence of the Lord in our lives. After Jesus went to Heaven to sit at the right hand of the Father, He provided that power to us through the Holy Spirit.

But you shall receive power when the Holy Spirit has come upon you; and you shall be witnesses to Me in Jerusalem, and in all Judea and Samaria, and to the end of the earth (Acts 1:8).

We need to make sure those we are discipling are filled with the Holy Spirit and recognize His power and Presence in their lives and ministry. We can only do the natural. He does the supernatural.

We need to make it very clear that believers cannot live a truly mature, effective, overcoming, victorious, and powerful Christian life until they are led by the Spirit of God. He is the One who gives us the power to change people's lives and circumstances. He is the One who bears witness to us that we truly are the sons and daughters of God. He is the One who guides us into all truth. And the ministry gifts He endows us with are essential to show others that the Kingdom of God is here among us.

Encourage

After we exhort, educate, and empower, there is one last E that is also very important. It is encouragement. Encouragement says, "You can do this!" Here is how the apostle Paul encouraged his disciple Timothy:

> *Let no one despise your youth, but be an example to the believers in word, in conduct, in love, in spirit, in faith, in purity. Till I come, give attention to reading, to exhortation, to doctrine. Do not neglect the gift that is in you, which was given to you by prophecy with the laying on of the hands of the eldership. Meditate on these things; give yourself entirely to them, that your progress may be evident to all. Take heed to yourself and to the doctrine. Continue in them, for in doing this you will save both yourself and those who hear you* (1 Timothy 4:12-16).

Many times we need to humble ourselves and let those we are mentoring know the struggles we went through to get to where we are now. In essence, "If I can do it, so can you." Too many times by putting on a good face or not sharing our challenges we discourage others. The power of our testimony can make the difference between success and failure for some. We need to let them know it is a process and they *will* get there. They need to know that *we* believe in *them*. Sometimes that is all it takes.

Just recently, a lady we have been ministering to told us that her walk with the Lord is better than it ever has been in her whole life. She said a big reason for that is because she knows we believe in her and value her. She felt like she had been put down and devalued all of her life by everyone she knew and never had anyone believe in her before, even though she had accomplished incredible things.

Someone truly believing in her and valuing her changed the way she saw herself and allowed her to understand that God believes in her and values her incredibly. That has benefitted her marriage, her children, her work situation, and all those around her. She now truly believes that she is God's favorite and it shows with the smile she wears on her face, where before there used to be tears and a frown.

Activate

The next step in this discipling process is to activate people. Jesus used this principle with the twelve disciples very effectively.

> *And when He had called His twelve disciples to Him, He gave them power over unclean spirits, to cast them out, and to heal all kinds of sickness and all kinds of disease* (Matthew 10:1).

> *And as you go, preach, saying, "The kingdom of heaven is at hand." Heal the sick, cleanse the lepers, raise the dead, cast out demons. Freely you have received, freely give* (Matthew 10:7-8).

While He was still with them and easily accessible, He sent them into all the towns and cities He was going to visit and allowed them to practice. Later He activated the seventy like He did the twelve. He did the same thing with water baptism.

Therefore, when the Lord knew that the Pharisees had heard that Jesus made and baptized more disciples than John (though Jesus Himself did not baptize, but His disciples) (John 4:1-2).

He gave them the opportunity to co-labor with Him while He was still there with them to mentor them. We need to do the same. When we see an opportunity to minister, we need to call someone we are discipling over and say, "Here, use what you have seen and heard, in the authority of Jesus, to minister to this person." I have done this many times since I learned this principle, and it is amazing the confidence it instills in people and the results it brings. Every time we do this we help people to have their own testimony of how God is using them. In order for a person to witness to others, they need to have testimonies of what God has done for and through them. When they have this, it is hard to keep silent. This was the testimony of the disciples when Jesus activated them:

Then the seventy returned with joy, saying, "Lord, even the demons are subject to us in Your name" (Luke 10:17).

I like to read between the lines on this verse. What I believe they were saying was, "Jesus, we were able to do all those things You told us to do—heal the sick, raise the dead, cast out devils, cleanse lepers, and tell the people that the Kingdom of Heaven is here. But we think the most exciting thing is that the demons were *subject* to *us* in Your name."

Jesus also used many occasions to correct the disciples when their way of thinking didn't line up with His. Here is an example of Jesus having to correct James and John, whom He called the Sons of Thunder, when their way of thinking was exactly opposite of what it needed to be.

> *Now it came to pass, when the time had come for Him to be received up, that He steadfastly set His face to go to Jerusalem, and sent messengers before His face. And as they went, they entered a village of the Samaritans, to prepare for Him. But they did not receive Him, because His face was set for the journey to Jerusalem. And when His disciples James and John saw this, they said, "Lord, do You want us to command fire to come down from heaven and consume them, just as Elijah did?" But He turned and rebuked them, and said, "You do not know what manner of spirit you are of. For the Son of Man did not come to destroy men's lives but to save them." And they went to another village* (Luke 9:51-56).

Jesus activated His disciples under the safety of His watchful eye, letting them do the ministry but making sure to guide them along the way. Activation is like the bumpers that bowling alleys use so that kids can learn to hit the pins without the frustration of the ball constantly going into the gutters. This way their confidence grows as they learn how to throw the ball accurately. When their instructors determine that they are ready, they remove the bumpers and let them go for it on their own.

Release

Release is the final stage of the discipling process. When Jesus felt the disciples were ready, He released them to do ministry under the guidance of the Holy Spirit. When we believe that our disciples are ready, we need to release them too. We know they are ready when we have given them all the training they need to be successful in fulfilling their mission and they are demonstrating Kingdom themselves. At this point we can entrust them to the Spirit of God and send them off to start the D.E.A.R. process with others. That isn't to say we won't be there for them if they need us, but at this point they have "graduated" to be mature ministers who are able to disciple others using the D.E.A.R. process themselves.

This is what Jesus said just before He ascended into Heaven:

> *And Jesus came and spoke to them, saying, "All authority has been given to Me in heaven and on earth. Go therefore and make disciples of all the nations, baptizing them in the name of the Father and of the Son and of the Holy Spirit, teaching them to observe all things that I have commanded you; and lo, I am with you always, even to the end of the age."* *Amen* (Matthew 28:18-20).

When God showed me this process, I was grieved because this wasn't the way I was discipled or had been discipling others myself. For many years now I have looked to Heaven and said to the Lord, "D.E.A.R. me Lord! D.E.A.R. me!" I was sincere, and He has been faithful to send people into my life who have *demonstrated, equipped, activated,* and then *released* me. Every time God shows me a new point of obedience, He is faithful to take me through D.E.A.R.

I believe we never arrive at the place where we outgrow the need to be somewhere in this process. A wise minister once said to me,

"You should always have both a Paul and Timothy in your life, no matter how mature you are as a Christian. We always need a person mentoring us and we should in turn be mentoring someone else."

The D.E.A.R. process requires that we are grounded in the fundamentals of the Word of God. In the next three chapters we will review those foundational principles again, offering insights that relate specifically to living a victorious supernatural life for the glory of God, full of signs, wonders, and miracles. These are things we learned over the course of our D.E.A.R. process from our previous pastors and teachers, our sojourn at Impact Church and Eastside Church, and also directly from the Holy Spirit who guides all of us into His truth.

We feel like we need to include these chapters in this book because we know our readers will be from all sorts of theological backgrounds and church denominations. We also know that each person, because of what they have been taught and their own experiences, sees these things through their own set of religious glasses. We want to create a common understanding to clear up any confusion as to what we believe the Spirit of Truth has revealed about these important topics.

We aren't holding ourselves up as biblical scholars, nor are we saying that we have secret biblical insights that have only been given to us. The Holy Spirit is consistently taking us through the D.E.A.R. process over and over again too. We just know that before we studied the Word through the spiritual lenses of what we knew to be true about God's nature and character and who we are in Him, we weren't living a supernatural life rich in signs, wonders, and miracles. So as you read these next three chapters, please be like the Bereans who:

Were more open-minded than those in Thessalonica, and they listened eagerly to Paul's message. They searched the Scriptures day after day to see if Paul and Silas were teaching the truth (Acts 17:11 NLT).

Chapter 10

LIVING HIS WORD

So the Word became human and made his home among us. He was full of unfailing love and faithfulness. And we have seen his glory, the glory of the Father's one and only Son (John 1:14 NLT).

JOE

The Word of God is essential to the victorious supernatural Christian life. It is the greatest weapon and resource that we have. It is the sword of the Spirit and a light unto our path and a lamp unto our feet. It will always accomplish what it was sent to do, and that is to defeat the enemy. It dispels his lies by showing us the pure truth. The Word is the blueprint from the Creator of our destiny. It is the map and the battle plan as well as the most powerful supernatural weapon that exists. Like a playbook for a football team that wins them the Super Bowl or a cookbook for master chefs that allows them to create great culinary masterpieces, it gives us the strategies we need to win the game of life and the steps to take to achieve our God-given destinies. It causes angels to come to our aid and demons to be exposed and run away when they hear us speak the Word of the Father into our situations.

If we aren't reading, hearing, or meditating on the Word every day, then we are doing ourselves a great injustice because we are depriving ourselves of the primary way our Lord speaks to us. He sent His Word to heal us (see Ps. 107:20), or in other words to give us total wholeness. He has given us everything we need for life and godliness (see 2 Pet. 1:3).

Jesus didn't just read, study, understand, speak, and live the Word; He is the Word. If we are destined to become like Him, then we need the Word to teach us how to do it. When Jesus was confronted by satan in the testing time He spent in the wilderness, He used the Word to counter the lies, half-truths, and misinterpretations of the Word that the enemy tempted Him with. If Jesus needed the Word to combat the enemy, how much more do we need it?

All Scripture is inspired by God and is useful to teach us what is true and to make us realize what is wrong in our lives. It corrects us when we are wrong and teaches us to do what is right. God uses it to prepare and equip his people to do every good work (2 Timothy 3:16-17 NLT).

Inspired means God breathed. What Paul was saying here is that all Scripture isn't from the mind of man but from the mind of God as He breathed His thoughts into those who penned His words. And it's not just some of the Scriptures; it's all of them. And just as Paul says here, the Word is active. It does things to us and for us if we read it with open hearts and let it do its mighty work.

As the apostle James writes:

> *But don't just listen to God's word. You must do what it says. Otherwise, you are only fooling yourselves* (James 1:22 NLT).

So let's enumerate the things Paul says in Second Timothy 3:16-17 about the Word that has come directly from the mind of our heavenly Father who loves us with an everlasting love and wants us to become just like His beloved Son, Jesus.

The Word of God

1. Teaches us what is true,

2. Makes us realize what is wrong in our lives,

3. Corrects us when we are wrong,

4. Teaches us to do what is right, and

5. Prepares us and equips us to do every good work.

Let's look again at the scripture about the Bereans from the last chapter:

And the people of Berea were more open-minded than those in Thessalonica, and they listened eagerly to Paul's message. They searched the Scriptures day after day to see if Paul and Silas were teaching the truth (Acts 17:11 NLT).

The Bereans, who lived at the same time as Paul, were commended by the Lord. First of all, when they heard the servants of God speak, they didn't immediately put up a wall or become offended or argue inside their minds so they could just disregard what was being said. They were open-minded and listened eagerly to what was being spoken.

Second, they didn't just accept what was being said as truth without checking it out. They were hearing something that might change their lives and wanted to make sure that what was said was absolutely true, so they went back to the only reliable source of truth, the Word of God. They searched (read, studied, researched, cross-referenced to other Old Testament scriptures, examined the words being used and their meanings, and took into account how the culture of the speaker or hearer had influence on the meaning of those words).

This gave them the opportunity to see if their thoughts and actions matched up to what was being said and gave them the opportunity to repent if they did not. Now the word repent, in theological terms, does not mean to tell someone you are sorry for something. It means to totally change your way of thinking so that it will totally change what you do from now on. That is what truly studying the Word does. It teaches us what is true and gives us an opportunity to repent and change our ways.

So let's look again at what Paul is telling Timothy about the Word of God.

1. It Teaches Us What Is True

We are surrounded by truths, pseudo-truths, falsehoods and outright lies. The enemy of our soul wants us to believe anything but the truth that the Lord wants to use to mold us into the image of Christ.

> *For whom he did foreknow, he also did predesti-*
> *nate to be conformed to the image of his Son, that*
> *he might be the firstborn among many brethren*
> (Romans 8:29 KJV).

If our ultimate destiny is to be conformed (molded) into the image (representation) of Jesus our Messiah, then we need to study the Word to see what that looks like. The Messiah is spoken about in the Old as well as the New Testament, so we need to read and meditate on both and let the Holy Spirit guide us.

This is what Jesus said about the Holy Spirit:

> *However, when He, the Spirit of truth, has come,*
> *He will guide you into all truth; for He will not*
> *speak on His own authority, but whatever He hears*
> *He will speak; and He will tell you things to come*
> (John 16:13).

Jesus says not only that the Holy Spirit will guide you into all truth, but that He will only speak what He hears and not on His own authority. So who is the Spirit hearing from? The same place that Jesus heard from:

> *I don't speak on my own authority. The Father who*
> *sent me has commanded me what to say and how to*
> *say it* (John 12:49 NLT).

So the Father is the ultimate source of truth. He is also the One who "inspired" the men who wrote the Holy Scriptures. So we see that if we want to know how to live life as the Father designed it for us, then we need to study the Word of God to find out what is true about living as a true son or daughter of God. Jesus also said:

> *But the Helper, the Holy Spirit, whom the Father*
> *will send in My name, He will teach you all things,*
> *and bring to your remembrance all things that I said*
> *to you* (John 14:26).

In order for the Spirit to bring the things that Jesus said back into our memory, we have to have the Scriptures in there in the first place. If we haven't read the words and committed them to memory, then there is nothing there for Him to bring back. In my own life, because of my daily meditation on the Word, it is natural for me to reflect on scriptures that apply to every situation that I'm in, and to speak those words out in faith and watch the Lord intervene.

The Holy Spirit uses the Word of God to identify the lies of the enemy and enlighten us to what the real truth is according to God. I would propose to you that this is the biggest problem that most Christians have. They don't really know what is true anymore. In the "Parable of the Wheat and the Tares," Jesus talks about what happens to the Word when we read it or hear it.

The kingdom of heaven is like a man who sowed good seed in his field. But while everyone was sleeping, his enemy came and sowed weeds among the wheat, and went away. When the wheat sprouted and formed heads, then the weeds also appeared (Matthew 13:24-26 NIV).

When truth is sown into us, our enemy, the devil, tries to plant his lies, misinformation, and half-truths to water down, confuse, or even negate that truth. If we don't truly study the Word to know it and meditate on it daily as it applies to our lives, then we won't be able to identify what is a lie and what is truth. It will be easier for us to let those weeds grow up with the true seeds of truth and make it ineffectual in our lives.

Paul says about those who truly know the Lord:

For we are not unaware of his [the devil's] *schemes* (2 Corinthians 2:11 NIV).

So we must be constantly vigilant to read, study, and meditate on the Word of God so it can teach us what is true and then act on what it teaches us.

2. Makes Us Realize What Is Wrong in Our Lives

To paraphrase what the apostle James said in James 1:22, if we just know truth, but don't apply it to ourselves, then we are foolish. One way the Word facilitates that is to shine the light of truth on our lives. I like to think of the Word as a spiritual black light. In the '70s black lights were very popular. It always intrigued me that the closer I got to the light, the more dust and lint I would see on myself, even on my skin.

I believe that applying the Word to our life acts just like that. At first, it exposes the little things that are easiest to change, but as we get deeper into the Word (i.e. closer to the black light) it exposes more things, such as the thoughts and the intents of our hearts, which are harder to identify and correct.

> *For the word of God is living and powerful, and sharper than any two-edged sword, piercing even to the division of soul and spirit, and of joints and marrow, and is a discerner of the thoughts and intents of the heart* (Hebrews 4:12).

As we allow the Word to transform our way of thinking, our lives change for the better. We understand that "His divine power has given us everything we need for a godly life through our knowledge of him who called us by his own glory and goodness" (2 Peter 1:3 NIV).

We can have hope because we know what the Lord has said about us:

> *"For I know the plans I have for you," declares the Lord, "plans to prosper you and not to harm you, plans to give you hope and a future"* (Jeremiah 29:11 NIV).

We have peace because we understand that as we allow the truth of the Word to identify the things that are wrong with our lives and we allow the Spirit of Truth to help us fix those things and we incorporate and walk in those truths, then our soul (mind, will, and emotions) prospers, and when it prospers our whole life becomes prosperous.

Beloved, I pray that you may prosper in all things and be in health, just as your soul prospers. For I rejoiced greatly when brethren came and testified of the truth that is in you, just as you walk in the truth (3 John 2-3).

3. Corrects Us When We Are Wrong

This may sound like the same thing as the previous section, but there is a subtle difference. While the Word is shining a floodlight over all our lives to show us what's wrong with them, it is also shining a spotlight every moment on our immediate thought life and the choices we are making every second. Some people would call that our conscience. Have you ever done something and felt swift conviction from the Holy Spirit? That is the spotlight of the Word when we aren't aligning with the nature and character of Jesus.

When the Word is so ingrained in us that it becomes part of our character, it can even stop us from thinking or doing things before they happen. I pray often that before I say something contrary to the truth, figuratively, my tongue would stick to the roof of my mouth. But if it does slide through, I'm more willing to repent in that moment and rectify what I've done before it becomes an offense.

4. Teaches Us to Do What Is Right

Not only does the Word teach us what is true and correct us when we are wrong, but it also teaches us to do what is right in the moment. Just because we know what is true, we may not be able to translate that into action.

*If anyone, then, knows the good they ought to do and
doesn't do it, it is sin for them* (James 4:17 NIV).

The Bible is full of stories and parables that show us how to
take the truth of the Word and use it to govern what we do in our
everyday circumstances. As we read about the triumphs and mis-
takes of others and see how the Lord lovingly praises and corrects
them as they are walking with Him, we can use that to show us
how to respond, rather than react, in the numerous daily situations
we are presented with in our lives. When we react, we usually do
that through emotion and pride and the result is usually a disaster.
When we respond correctly, with reflection upon His Word and
what He would say and do, then it is redemptive to the person and
the situation.

5. Prepares Us and Equips Us to Do Every Good Work

And not only does the Word of God teach us to do what is
right in our challenging situations, it also prepares us and equips
us to become like Jesus:

> *Who went about doing good and healing all who
> were oppressed by the devil, for God was with Him*
> (Acts 10:38).

He not only wants us to respond to situations with the Word,
He wants us to incorporate His Word into our very being and
make it who we are. As Jesus re-presented the Father, so He wants
us to re-present Him to the world.

> *Jesus answered: "Don't you know me, Philip, even
> after I have been among you such a long time?*

Anyone who has seen me has seen the Father" (John 14:9 NIV).

Jesus, who is the embodiment of the Word itself, wants us to be like Him. The Father designed us to be like Him—to be the living Word to our generation, saying and doing only what He says to say and do.

As the apostle John says:

Love has been perfected among us in this: that we may have boldness in the day of judgment; because as He is, so are we in this world (1 John 4:17).

Paul puts it beautifully as he is talking about how he lived the Word in front of the Corinthians. Because of that their lives became a testimony of living the Word to others:

You yourselves are our letter, written on our hearts, known and read by everyone. You show that you are a letter from Christ, the result of our ministry, written not with ink but with the Spirit of the living God, not on tablets of stone but on tablets of human hearts (2 Corinthians 3:2-3 NIV).

The Father is calling us to re-present Jesus to the world. We are to live a life that exemplifies who we are in Him. Will you take the challenge to truly live the Word by studying it as though it were the basis of a victorious, supernatural Kingdom life? Because that is what the Word is. It shows us how to become like Jesus, and that is your God-designed destiny.

Chapter 11

BEING FILLED WITH HIS SPIRIT

I am going to send you what my Father has promised;
but stay in the city until you have been clothed with
power from on high (Luke 24:49 NIV).

JOE

I felt like we needed to include this chapter on the game changing promise Jesus made to His disciples just before He went back
to Heaven. There are so many opinions and so much disinforma-
tion that we wanted to try to clarify what we believe the truth is

about the "baptism" in the Holy Spirit. But first we need to lay a foundation.

Let's start with a look at who the Holy Spirit is:

1. He is an equal part of the divine Godhead along with the Father and the Son (Matt. 28:19-20).

2. He is the power of God (Acts 1:8; Zech. 4:6; Mic. 3:8; Rom. 15:13, 19).

3. He was an active participant in the Creation (Gen. 1:2).

4. He is referred to by many names including Holy Spirit, Holy Ghost, Spirit of the Lord, Spirit of God, and Spirit of Christ.

5. He guarantees our inheritance in the Kingdom (Eph. 1:14).

6. He witnesses to our spirit that we are the children of God (Rom. 8:16).

7. He guides us into all truth (John 16:13).

8. He teaches us all things and brings to our remembrance everything the Lord has said to us (John 14:26).

9. He does not speak with His own authority, but only what He hears from the Father (John 16:13).

10. He convicts the world of sin and righteousness (John 16:5).

The Holy Spirit in the Old Testament

Some people believe that the Holy Spirit is only active in the New Testament. Nothing could be further from the truth. Let's list some of the places in the Old Testament where the Holy Spirit is seen in His power and glory.

As we said above, He is a vital part of creating everything there is (see Gen. 1:2; Job 26:13; Isa. 32:15). He is the one who gives life to man and all the rest of God's creatures.

> *And the Lord God formed man of the dust of the ground, and breathed into his nostrils the breath of life; and man became a living being* (Genesis 2:7).

Note that the word *breath* that is used here is translated other places as *spirit*.

The Spirit strives with man in Genesis 6:3, which mirrors His work of convicting people of sin, righteousness, and judgment that we see in John 16:8-11.

> *And the Lord said, "My Spirit shall not strive with man forever, for he is indeed flesh"* (Genesis 6:3).

> *When he comes, he will prove the world to be in the wrong about sin and righteousness and judgment: about sin, because people do not believe in me; about righteousness, because I am going to the Father, where you can see me no longer; and about judgment, because the prince of this world now stands condemned* (John 16:8-11 NIV).

In the Old Testament the Spirit came upon prophets, kings, judges, and warriors in a way that gave them supernatural power for prophecy, wisdom, great exploits, signs, wonders, and miracles.

Moses says to his leaders, "And the Lord said to Moses: 'Take Joshua the son of Nun with you, a man in whom is the Spirit, and lay your hand on him'" (Num. 27:18).

It says about Othniel, one of Israel's first judges, "The Spirit of the Lord came upon him, and he judged Israel" (Judg. 3:10).

About Gideon, another of Israel's judges whom the Lord used to free His people from bondage, "But the Spirit of the Lord came upon Gideon; then he blew the trumpet, and the Abiezrites gathered behind him" (Judg. 6:34).

Describing Samson, probably the most well-known and the strongest of all of the judges of Israel, "And the Spirit of the Lord came mightily upon him, and he tore the lion apart as one would have torn apart a young goat, though he had nothing in his hand" (Judg. 14:6).

About Saul, who was anointed the first king over all of Israel, "When they came there to the hill, there was a group of prophets to meet him; then the Spirit of God came upon him, and he prophesied among them" (1 Sam. 10:10).

King David declares in Second Samuel 23:2, "the Spirit of the Lord spoke by me, and His word was on my tongue." And in Psalm 51:11 he pleads, "Do not cast me away from Your presence, and do not take Your Holy Spirit from me."

First Chronicles 12:18 says, "Then the Spirit came upon [literally, 'clothed'] Amasai, chief of the captains, and he said: 'We are yours, O David; we are on your side, O son of Jesse!'"

The prophet Ezekiel proclaims, "The Spirit entered me when He spoke to me" (Ezek. 2:2).

The prophet Micah announces, "But truly I am full of power by the Spirit of the Lord, and of justice and might, to declare to Jacob his transgression and to Israel his sin" (Mic. 3:8).

The whole Bible, both Old and New Testaments together, are one story—a beautiful tapestry portraying the Messiah Jesus. His threads are interwoven into every book, every chapter, and every verse. It is, if you will, His-Story, a prophetic manuscript all about who He is and His relationship to us, and it is the Holy Spirit who reveals Him to us and through us.

Now let me define prophecy. Prophecy can be foretelling, forth-telling, or both. Foretelling is prophesying about future events. Forth-telling is prophesying what the Lord has said or is saying currently about a person, place, or situation. The preaching of the Gospel is an example of prophetic forth-telling because it is speaking a word of exhortation or encouragement to another person or persons.

So if we look at the Bible in that understanding of prophecy, then we can see that it is full of both foretelling and forth-telling.

Above all, you must realize that no prophecy in Scripture ever came from the prophet's own understanding, or from human initiative. No, those prophets were moved by the Holy Spirit, and they spoke from God (2 Peter 1:20-21 NLT).

One of the things that the Holy Spirit did in the Old Testament was to foretell about the coming of the Messiah, the Anointed One, who would redeem humanity and reconcile us back to the

Father. This was needed to close the great gulf that was formed between God and mankind because of Adam's sin in the Garden of Eden. In some Bibles, the editors will put a star or some other notation beside verses that proclaim the Messiah.

Without these foretelling prophetic words, Mary wouldn't have understood the significance of what the angel was saying to her when he announced that she would be the one to give birth to the Messiah. The shepherds wouldn't have been excited about the angelic proclamation about the Savior. The wise men wouldn't have known to look for a sign or what the star meant. The king's scribes wouldn't have known where to tell Herod the baby Messiah was to be born. John the Baptist, who was the forerunner of Jesus, wouldn't have made any sense to the people of Israel. Simeon wouldn't have understood his own prophecy about the Lord's salvation, and Anna would have been perplexed about why he was so excited. And the scribes, Pharisees, Sadducees, and the Jewish people wouldn't have known what Jesus was talking about when He spoke of who He was and why He came.

One of the things that we see about the Spirit in the Old Testament is that He would "come upon" people, empowering them only when the Lord needed them to do something supernatural and then He would "leave" them, or actually He would remove that empowerment. Jesus changed all of that when He came, and that is where it gets even more exciting for us.

The Abiding Presence of the Holy Spirit

I heard Bill Johnson say, "The Holy Spirit is in us for us, but He is on us for others." I don't believe that he was talking about the literal location of the Holy Spirit, but really about the Spirit's

Presence in us to confirm who we are in Him and guide us into all truth versus His anointing and empowerment upon our lives for supernatural ministry to others.

Jesus, after His resurrection, appears to His disciples and says:

> *"As the Father has sent me, so I am sending you."*
> *Then he breathed on them and said, "Receive the*
> *Holy Spirit. If you forgive anyone's sins, they are*
> *forgiven. If you do not forgive them, they are not*
> *forgiven"* (John 20:21-23 NLT).

But in Acts 1:4 He says, "Do not leave Jerusalem until the Father sends you the gift he promised, as I told you before. John baptized with water, but in just a few days you will be baptized with the Holy Spirit" (NLT).

Wait a minute. They had already received the Holy Spirit, but now He is telling them that there is another experience with the Spirit that they need? In verse 8 He explains it a little more:

> *But you will receive power when the Holy Spirit*
> *comes upon you* (Acts 1:8 NLT).

So, let's see, they "received" the Holy Spirit first, which made them true children of God giving them authority to do what only God can do (see Mark 2:7). And then they were "baptized" later to give them the power (*dunamis*) to do it.

Let's look at Jesus. He was born the Son of God, and His Spirit is the Holy Spirit. (Remember, one of the names of the Holy Spirit is the Spirit of Christ.) So why didn't He walk in the supernatural until He was about 30 years old? What event happened in His life that made the difference?

When all the people were baptized, it came to pass that Jesus also was baptized; and while He prayed, the heaven was opened. And the Holy Spirit descended in bodily form like a dove upon Him, and a voice came from heaven which said, "You are My beloved Son; in You I am well pleased" (Luke 3:21-22).

The apostle John records an important difference in this instance of the Holy Spirit coming upon a person.

I saw the Spirit descending from heaven like a dove, and He remained upon Him. I did not know Him, but He who sent me to baptize with water said to me, "Upon whom you see the Spirit descending, and remaining on Him, this is He who baptizes with the Holy Spirit." And I have seen and testified that this is the Son of God (John 1:32-34).

This is the difference between the Old and the New Testament. Now the Spirit would come and remain. Jesus restored what Adam had lost—the abiding Presence of the Spirit of God upon man. I believe this is why Jesus didn't do any miraculous things until He was baptized (clothed, covered, immersed) in the Holy Spirit. That was when He was empowered. He was foreshadowing that the same thing would happen to us. First, we would receive the Holy Spirit when we repent and follow Him as Savior and Lord (salvation), and then we would be empowered when we are baptized in the Spirit, and He would remain upon us.

Let's see what Jesus quotes from the Book of Isaiah when He is asked to read in the synagogue:

The Spirit of the Lord is upon me, for he has anointed me to bring Good News to the poor. He has sent me to proclaim that captives will be released, that the blind will see, that the oppressed will be set free, and that the time of the Lord's favor has come (Luke 4:18-19 NLT).

Jesus also said to His disciples, us being included, *"Peace be with you. As the Father has sent me, so I am sending you"* (John 20:21 NLT).

So we not only need the Presence of the Holy Spirit within us, we also need His power upon us to live as true supernatural Kingdom children of our heavenly Father, just as Jesus did.

The Baptism of the Holy Spirit

There has been a lot of debate about the nature of the baptism of the Holy Spirit. I'm not going to try to discuss all of the different views about what it is, when it happens, or what it looks like. I'm just going to give you what I believe the Spirit gave me to help you to understand it better. My comment to people when they ask me about how to be baptized, or "filled," with the Spirit is this: "It isn't about how much of the Holy Spirit you have; it's how much of you the Holy Spirit has. There is no big or little Holy Spirit. He comes in His totality and not in pieces. There is no junior Holy Spirit for children and a senior Holy Spirit for adults. The empowerment comes when you give Him rights to every part of you so He can trust you with His supernatural power."

First, let's look at the word baptism as it pertains to the baptism of the Holy Spirit. The Greek word for baptism in this case is *baptizo*, which means to dip repeatedly, immerse, submerge, or overwhelm. This isn't to be confused with another Greek word for baptism which is *bapto*, which means to dip only once.

An example of both of these words is in a recipe for making pickles from the Greek poet and physician Nicander who lived in about 200 B.C. He states that in order to make the recipe, the small cucumbers need to be dipped (bapto) in boiling water and then submerged (baptizo) in the vinegar solution. The first baptism (bapto) is temporary and affects just the outside skin of the cucumbers. It makes it ready for what comes next. The second baptism (baptizo) produces a permanent change as the prolonged immersion in the vinegar solution saturates and permeates the cucumber to its very core. It changes the very nature of the thing that is being baptized and now it is called a pickle. We no longer call it a cucumber. That is why, in many cases, the word baptism is used interchangeably with "being filled" with the Spirit. Everything within us has a new nature and we don't look or respond the same as before.

I have used another visual aid when I have preached about being filled with the Spirit. I take two identical clear glasses. One is totally empty and the other is filled with marbles. I pour blue colored water into the empty glass to signify being filled with the Spirit. The total appearance of the glass becomes solid blue as the liquid completely fills the inside of the vessel it was poured into. This is a picture of someone who has emptied themselves of everything that is carnal and worldly and allows the Holy Spirit to be the only source of their thoughts, words, and actions.

Jesus, who was our model of being filled with the Spirit, said:

> *Very truly I tell you, the Son can do nothing by himself;*
> *he can do only what he sees his Father doing, because*

whatever the Father does the Son also does. For the Father loves the Son and shows him all he does. Yes, and he will show him even greater works than these, so that you will be amazed (John 5:19-20 NIV).

The Spirit of the Lord had total reign in the life of Jesus, so much that He did nothing unless He saw the Father doing it. Jesus emptied Himself so the Holy Spirit could have full control. Paul says about Jesus:

Who, being in very nature God, did not consider equality with God something to be used to his own advantage; rather, he made himself nothing by taking the very nature of a servant, being made in human likeness. And being found in appearance as a man, he humbled himself by becoming obedient to death— even death on a cross! (Philippians 2:6-8 NIV)

Next, I pour the blue liquid from that now full glass into the glass that is full of something else—marbles in this case. The marbles signify the things we have in our lives that aren't godly, but carnal and self-seeking. These could represent pride, fear, anger, bitterness, unforgiveness, selfishness, greed, hate, and so many other things that are all about us. When I'm done filling this glass to its top, even though it looks full there is so much more still left in the first glass. The new glass is really not totally full of what we were hoping would be there, because there are other things in the way.

In order for that glass to be full, I start getting rid of the marbles. I name them as I take them out to show what we need to remove to make our vessel unencumbered by the carnal ungodly nature so that we can truly be filled with the Spirit. When I'm finished taking out all those things, then I can pour in the rest from the other glass, which is now empty, signifying that now this new glass is totally full.

Paul gives this command, "Do not get drunk on wine, which leads to debauchery. Instead, be filled with the Spirit" (Eph. 5:18 NIV).

Instead of allowing something else to take control of you so that you become carnal and ungodly, be filled with the Spirit. I have been told that the Greek syntax for "be filled" actually has the meaning of "be being filled," a continual process that we have to be aware of every day so that other stuff doesn't sneak back in.

Why Is Being Filled with the Holy Spirit so Important?

We have already said that we need the empowerment of the Spirit to be able to live the true Christian life and do the supernatural things such as healing the sick, raising the dead, casting out devils, and cleansing lepers to demonstrate that the Kingdom of Heaven is here. We also need Him for the gifts He brings and the fruit we bear when He has full control of our lives.

> *There are diversities of gifts, but the same Spirit distributes them. Now to each one the manifestation of the Spirit is given for the common good. To one there is given through the Spirit a message of wisdom, to another a message of knowledge by means of the same Spirit, to another faith by the same Spirit, to another gifts of healing by that one Spirit, to another miraculous powers, to another prophecy, to another distinguishing between spirits,*

to another speaking in different kinds of tongues, and to still another the interpretation of tongues. All these are the work of one and the same Spirit, and he distributes them to each one, just as he determines (1 Corinthians 12:4, 7-11 NIV).

But the fruit of the Spirit is love, joy, peace, long-suffering, kindness, goodness, faithfulness, gentleness, self-control. Against such there is no law (Galatians 5:22-23).

The Holy Spirit Gives Us Boldness to Preach God's Word

Peter and John were walking to the Temple one day and saw a lame man at the Gate Beautiful. He was begging for money, but instead of giving him a few alms:

Peter said, "Silver and gold I do not have, but what I do have I give you: In the name of Jesus Christ of Nazareth, rise up and walk." And he took him by the right hand and lifted him up, and immediately his feet and ankle bones received strength. So he, leaping up, stood and walked and entered the temple with them—walking, leaping, and praising God. And all the people saw him walking and praising God. Then they knew that it was he who sat begging alms at the Beautiful Gate of the temple; and they were filled with wonder and amazement at what had happened to him (Acts 3:6-10).

Peter and John used this miracle as an opportunity to preach the good news about Jesus the Messiah. This got them in big

trouble with the Sanhedrin, the very rulers who had Jesus cruci-
fied. When they were arrested and called to defend their actions
of speaking in the name of Jesus, they boldly preached the Gospel
to the leaders themselves. When those leaders saw the boldness of
Peter and John, they noted that these men had been with Jesus.
Because the man who had been healed was standing next to the
disciples, they could say nothing against the miracle, so the leaders
commanded the disciples not to preach in the name of Jesus. Peter
and John replied to them:

> *"Whether it is right in the sight of God to listen to
> you more than to God, you judge. For we cannot but
> speak the things which we have seen and heard." So
> when they had further threatened them, they let them
> go, finding no way of punishing them, because of the
> people, since they all glorified God for what had been
> done* (Acts 4:19-21).

Peter and John then went back to the rest of the disciples and
reported what had happened. Now here is the interesting part to
me. This was the first time the disciples had the boldness to preach
to the leaders of the Jewish people and they recognized that it was
the miracle that gave them that boldness, so they prayed:

> *Now, Lord, look on their threats, and grant to Your
> servants that with all boldness they may speak Your
> word, by stretching out Your hand to heal, and that
> signs and wonders may be done through the name of
> Your holy Servant Jesus* (Acts 4:29-30).

And the Lord answered them like this:

And when they had prayed, the place where they were assembled together was shaken; and they were all filled with the Holy Spirit, and they spoke the word of God with boldness (Acts 4:31).

The Lord filled them *again* with the Holy Spirit to empower them to do the supernatural things that proved that Jesus was the Messiah, and because of that they were able to speak God's Word with renewed boldness.

The Spirit of the Lord Prays Through Us

There is one thing the Holy Spirit does that I believe we cannot do without and still live a victorious supernatural Christian life:

And the Holy Spirit helps us in our weakness. For example, we don't know what God wants us to pray for. But the Holy Spirit prays for us with groanings that cannot be expressed in words. And the Father who knows all hearts knows what the Spirit is saying, for the Spirit pleads for us believers in harmony with God's own will (Romans 8:26-27 NLT).

The Holy Spirit helps us when we are weak, and if you are anything like me that is quite often. He prays through us, for us. Sometimes He prays in our own language, sometimes in another known tongue or unknown heavenly language, and sometimes with sounds that cannot be expressed with any words at all. I cannot tell you the times that we didn't know what to pray, and we allowed the Spirit of God to pray through us and the things we needed came or the situation that looked hopeless turned around.

Paul says in First Corinthians 14:18, "I thank my God I speak with tongues more than you all." He had given the Holy Spirit his voice, his "tongue" if you will—that thing that seems to be the hardest for us to control. As James says:

> But no human being can tame the tongue. It is a restless evil, full of deadly poison (James 3:8 NIV).

Paul knew the power of allowing the Holy Spirit to have full control of his life, his tongue, and his destiny.

HEIDI

Don't ever underestimate the power of praying in the Spirit. This is just one of those things that cannot be explained or fully understood. It is supernatural and the supernatural is just that, "super-natural"—in other words, not natural. Our heavenly Father asks us to do the natural so He can accomplish the supernatural through us like a heavenly conduit. We are all familiar with the expression, "We are His hands and feet." We are also His mouthpiece. Aligning our thoughts, our actions, and our speech with Him creates a very powerful connection with the King of Kings. When that occurs the stage is set to accomplish His Word.

About 20 years ago, in the middle of the day, I was at home, homeschooling my youngest son Joshua. It was time to get ready and head out the door to pick up my middle son Jonathan from school, which was a 35-minute drive one way. Unexplainably, this heaviness came over me and I knew it was time to pray. I had no idea what I was praying about, so I began to pray in the Spirit.

There are times when I pray in the Spirit that I get an idea of sorts, or a vision, of what I'm praying for. However, that didn't happen this time. I started praying about 2:10 in the afternoon. I drove into town, got Jonathan, and continued to pray in the Spirit all the way home. I got home, unloaded the van of kids and book bags, and right around 3:35 the heaviness lifted just as quickly as it came. I still had no idea what that was all about. My heart was glad that I was obedient, but I was curious as to what or who I was interceding for, knowing full well that I just might never know this side of Heaven.

I had all but forgotten about the situation by the following day, but then a family member called me that evening. I was quite concerned because it was rare for him to call. He said that he and his family were very upset. I asked what happened, and he told me that his teenage son was in a car accident the day before and, though he sustained minor injuries, his son's best friend, who was with him, died after being thrown from the vehicle. We talked for another 20 minutes and I did my best to console him. It wasn't until 20 to 30 minutes later that I realized that not once was the time of the accident mentioned. I had to find out. Calling back, I asked when the accident occurred. "Around 3:30 in the afternoon," was their response.

I shared the reason I had asked, and then told them I had been praying yesterday for over an hour and didn't know why, but now I did. It was explained to me that there were three people in a pickup truck and no one was wearing a seatbelt. One man was at the wheel, the son of the man I was talking to was in the middle, and his friend was beside him next to the passenger door. The vehicle in front of them swerved sharply to miss something on the freeway at 70 MPH. The driver of their truck overcorrected and caused the truck to roll over several times in the median. The man's son was hurt, but was able to get out of the truck. What the son couldn't explain was that while the truck was rolling, he felt like someone or something was holding him in place while he ducked down. He should have been thrown all around the cab or even out of the cab.

I believe that it was an angel holding him in place because of the power of prayer. The Holy Spirit knew what was happening at that time, but I couldn't have known. He prayed the prayer of intercession through me to keep that family member safe from what could have been his untimely death.

JOE

Jesus, the only begotten Son of God, who is our Model, Savior, and Teacher, needed the Holy Spirit to be upon Him to complete His mission and fulfill His divine purpose here on earth. If He needed that, then we, all the more, need the Holy Spirit to be upon us, in us, and saturating us completely to complete our mission and to fulfill our God-designed destinies.

Chapter 12

AT HOME IN HIS PRESENCE

He who dwells in the secret place of the Most High shall abide under the shadow of the Almighty. I will say of the Lord, "He is my refuge and my fortress; my God, in Him I will trust" (Psalm 91:1-2).

JOE

Now let's turn our attention to another one of the important aspects of living the supernatural, overcoming Christian life. One that I believe has been given too little emphasis in the past, but is beginning to make its way back into the Church. I'm speaking of the Father's desire that we abide in His Presence. To be reconciled to Him in such a way that we spend quality time with Him in a very deep personal relationship. To be one with Him as Jesus prayed for us to be:

> *I am praying not only for these disciples but also for all who will ever believe in me through their message. I pray that they will all be one, just as you and I are one—as you are in me, Father, and I am in you. And may they be in us so that the world will believe you sent me.*
>
> *I have given them the glory you gave me, so they may be one as we are one. I am in them and you are in me. May they experience such perfect unity that the world will know that you sent me and that you love them as much as you love me* (John 17:20-23 NLT).

This place of abiding in His Presence has many different names in both the Old and New Testaments. It is called:

- The secret place, the shadow of the Almighty, and our refuge and fortress in Psalm 91;

- Dwelling in the house of the Lord in Psalm 23:6;

- The cover of His Presence in Psalm 31:20;

- God's place of rest in Exodus 33:14 and Hebrews 4:9-11;

- The Holy of Holies in Exodus 26:31-33;

- In perfect peace in Isaiah 26:3;

▪ Abiding in the vine in John 15:1-10.

Psalm 91 is one of my favorite chapters of the Bible. I have committed it to memory and quote it aloud to myself all the time. This was one Psalm that was my mainstay during the time I was so ill. It is a Psalm filled with incredible promises to the believer and is the essence of the Gospel itself. It was written about the Messiah, but because we are joint heirs with Jesus it applies to us as His children also. I encourage you to memorize this Psalm so it can be your "go to" scripture when you are in trouble yourself.

Psalm 91

> *He who dwells in the secret place of the Most High*
> *Shall abide under the shadow of the Almighty.*
> *I will say of the Lord, "He is my refuge and my*
> *fortress; My God, in Him I will trust."*
> *Surely He shall deliver you from the snare of the*
> *fowler and from the perilous pestilence.*
> *He shall cover you with His feathers,*
> *And under His wings you shall take refuge;*
> *His truth shall be your shield and buckler.*
> *You shall not be afraid of the terror by night,*
> *Nor of the arrow that flies by day,*
> *Nor of the pestilence that walks in darkness,*
> *Nor of the destruction that lays waste at noonday.*
> *A thousand may fall at your side,*
> *And ten thousand at your right hand;*
> *But it shall not come near you.*
> *Only with your eyes shall you look,*
> *And see the reward of the wicked.*

Because you have made the Lord, who is my refuge,
Even the Most High, your dwelling place,
No evil shall befall you,
Nor shall any plague come near your dwelling;
For He shall give His angels charge over you,
To keep you in all your ways.
In their hands they shall bear you up,
Lest you dash your foot against a stone.
You shall tread upon the lion and the cobra,
The young lion and the serpent
you shall trample underfoot.
"Because he has set his love upon Me,
therefore I will deliver him;
I will set him on high,
because he has known My name.
He shall call upon Me, and I will answer him;
I will be with him in trouble;
I will deliver him and honor him.
With long life I will satisfy him,
And show him My salvation."

As I was quoting this psalm to the Lord one day, He impressed on me to quote the first sentence again. "He who dwells in the secret place of the Most High shall abide under the shadow of the Almighty." At that moment I realized something that had eluded me in the past. All the promises of safety, blessing, healing, and protection were all based on obedience to that first sentence, "He who dwells."

That word dwell is the Hebrew word *yashab*, which means "to sit, to remain, to dwell, to abide; causatively, to settle, to make your home, to take up permanent residence, to marry."

These incredible promises of God are only valid if we make our home in His Presence. We can't count on any of this unless we find out how to "dwell in that secret place."

Some of the most incredible people in the Bible are the ones that were able to be at home in His Presence. Enoch walked with God, and then he disappeared, because God took him. Noah found grace in the eyes of the Lord. Abraham was called the friend of God, and God consulted with him. Moses met with God "face to face." David wrote the 23rd Psalm out of his experience with the Good Shepherd. Isaiah saw the Lord high and lifted up and His glory filling the temple, and was so in tune with God at that point that he overheard a conversation the Godhead was having. Paul was taken up into the third heaven and saw things he couldn't describe. John was in the Spirit on the Lord's Day and through that vision wrote the Book of Revelation. And of course Jesus lived so much in the Presence of God that He didn't say anything unless He heard the Father saying it or do anything unless He saw the Father doing it—re-presenting the Father as His perfect image.

It has been observed that we tend to look and act like the people we spend the most time with. This is certainly true when we spend time in the Presence of God. The disciples, as we have discussed before, certainly looked like Jesus, because the Pharisees noted that they had been with Him. Go back and look at Psalm 91. Can you see the overcoming, victorious life it describes there? We can only have that life if we spend time in His Presence.

Before we go on, I would like to take a small detour to give us a basis for our journey into His Presence.

The Nature and the Character of God

The nature of God is His substance, His essence, and His unique qualities. It is what makes Him holy, set apart from His creation. As He Himself proclaims:

> *Thus says the Lord, the King of Israel, and his Redeemer, the Lord of hosts: "I am the First and I am the Last; besides Me there is no God"* (Isaiah 44:6).

There is no one else but God who is immortal, eternal, infinite, self-existent, self-determinant (He has total, perfect free will), unchangeable, infinitely moral, immutable, perfect, all-powerful, all-knowing, and ever-present.

The character of God is why He does what He does. Because of His nature, He could have chosen anything as His motivation. His choice would become His standard, His perfect "moral law" for the way He expresses Himself toward everything, especially toward His creation. Of all the things God could have chosen for Himself, He made an incredible and infinitely profound decision. He chose love.

God is love (1 John 4:8,16).

The Greek word used here is *agape*. It is defined as "a decision of the will, to promote the good of another, expecting nothing in return." This kind of love, which defines God's character, is infinite, voluntary, free, intelligent, virtuous, not selfish or self-seeking, impartial, universal, efficient, opposed to sin, compassionate, merciful, just, true, patient, kind, meek, holy, and wise. As the apostle Paul wrote:

> *Love is patient, love is kind. It does not envy, it does not boast, it is not proud. It does not dishonor others, it is not self-seeking, it is not easily angered, it keeps no record of wrongs. Love does not delight in evil but rejoices with the truth. It always protects, always trusts, always hopes, always perseveres. Love never fails* (1 Corinthians 13:4-8 NIV).

God's love is perfect and He chose us to be the object of His affection. One of the most quoted verses in the Bible is John 3:16.

> *For God so loved the world that He gave His only begotten Son, that whoever believes in Him should not perish but have everlasting life.*

Because God loves us, He wants us to be with Him forever. He wants an intimate personal relationship with us. He wants to shower us with His divine goodness. But the only way He could do that after the fall of man was to pay the penalty of that crime Himself. The sentence was death, so He sacrificed Himself on the cross though the person of His Son Jesus. This is how intensely He loves us and the extreme measures He was willing take to have us in His Presence for eternity.

How We Come into His Presence

There are many ways we can come into the Presence of the Lord. I will speak here about the way King David, a man after God's own heart, felt was the most honoring to God. By following

David's instructions, we can have the right heart and mind as we enter in. David writes:

Make a joyful shout to the Lord, all you lands! Serve the Lord with gladness; come before His presence with singing. Know that the Lord, He is God; it is He who has made us, and not we ourselves; we are His people and the sheep of His pasture.

Enter into His gates with thanksgiving, and into His courts with praise. Be thankful to Him, and bless His name. For the Lord is good; His mercy is everlasting, and His truth endures to all generations (Psalm 100).

Within these verses there are many nuggets that show us the thoughts, emotions, attitudes, and actions that we should have as we endeavor to come into His Presence. In this Psalm, David is making reference to how the people of Israel were to come in the Temple, through its various areas and rooms, and into the Holy of Holies where the Presence of the Lord manifested on the earth at that time. I'm not going to go into a lengthy discussion on the Temple. Other people have written entire books on that subject. So let's look at its basic structure as it pertains to our subject here.

The Temple had many gates that led into it. All the gates had names, like the Eastern Gate, the Beautiful Gate, the Music Gate, the Sacrifice Gate, and many more. These gates led into courts, which were large areas where people could gather. Within the inner court, where the sacrifices were made, there were twelve steps that led up into the Holy Place. Beyond the Holy Place, behind a heavy veil (curtain) was the Holy of Holies.

The only person who was allowed to go into the Holy of Holies was the High Priest who was only allowed to go in once every year. In order for him to be allowed to go in, he had to be pure and blameless through a rigorous set of rituals he had to perform. So important was the way he entered the Presence of God that if he didn't do it absolutely perfectly, he would be struck dead and have to be pulled out by a rope tied around his ankle. Fortunately for us, when Jesus died that curtain was torn in two to show that we can come boldly before His Presence where we find His mercy and His grace (see Heb. 4:16).

But this boldness, which is the confidence we have in Jesus that we won't be rejected, has turned into other attitudes. These attitudes have become detrimental to our ability to come into His Presence correctly and stay there. This ungodly boldness has turned into pride, arrogance, impatience, selfishness, duty, and unbelief.

Some people spend their prayer time like they are going to a fast food restaurant and ordering a hamburger, fries, and a large drink. They demand prompt service because they have given their time and money and expect God to respond to their requests immediately. The only time they come to Him is when they need something and never really want to just be with Him and enjoy His Presence. Others, out of duty, spend their five minutes acknowledging God's existence, go through their list of requests, and then get up and walk away to go throughout their day doing everything on their own. Even if God does intervene in their circumstances, they never acknowledge it was Him.

Many don't have faith enough to even try to connect with God or they just don't have the time. I love what Clara, one of the characters in the movie War Room, replies to Elizabeth when she says she doesn't have time to go to God in prayer every day about her marital problems. "But you apparently have time to fight losing battles with your husband," she exclaims. God wants to be involved in every area of our lives. Jesus came so we could have abundant life, but that won't happen if we don't spend time with the One who has the power to make it so.

If we would just understand that in Him we live and move and have our being (see Acts 17:28 NIV) and that if we seek Him we will find Him if we seek Him with all of our hearts (see Jer. 29:13), we would approach Him totally differently. Let's see how David says we should do it.

Enter into His Gates with Thanksgiving

In order to get into a place, we must enter through the door—in this case the gate. David says we should do so with thankfulness. He clarifies that this thankfulness needs to be directed toward the Lord. So why does he say that in order to get through the door we must be thankful? When we are thankful, we are showing our gratitude for something someone has done for us. It is usually something that we don't feel we have a right to. We feel grateful to that person because they didn't have to do it, but they did. We speak the thing out loud and embrace them to show our sincerity. It is a stance of humility as we express honor to the one who has blessed us.

I'm talking about really being thankful, not about feeling like you have to because your mom or dad told you that was the right thing to do. This posture takes away arrogance and pride. It quenches the feeling that we deserve something just because of who we are. It corrects our posture and places us in the position to be ready for the next step.

And Into His Courts with Praise

Let me make what I believe is the distinction between thankfulness and praise. As we said, thankfulness is being grateful for something someone has done specifically for you. Praise is expressing admiration for someone's character qualities or achievements whether or not it has directly affected you in some way. Thankfulness is personal. Praise is general. The picture of praise is standing with your hands raised indicating adoration. Because of this, praise takes us deeper into humility and raises the value of God as someone worthy to be praised regardless of whether His goodness directly affects us or not. He is worthy of our love, respect, and admiration just because of who He is. When we shout or sing the word "hallelujah" to the Lord, we are literally saying, in Hebrew, "Praise Jehovah," which is praising His Holy name.

Bless His Name

Verse 4 of Psalm 100 also tells us to "bless His Name," which is part of both praise and worship. The Hebrew word here is *barak*, which means "to kneel as an act of adoration." God has revealed the attributes of His love for us through the names by which He calls Himself. When Moses asked God His name, God responded with JHVH, which is translated, "I AM that I AM" or "the Self Existent One." Theologians aren't sure how this name is pronounced because the Jewish people stopped speaking that name of God out loud. They felt it was too holy. The closest pronunciation is either Jehovah or Yahweh. The New King James Version of the Bible uses Jehovah, so I will use that here too.

The Bible is full of references to the names of God. Some names include the Hebrew name for God, which is *El*, and others begin with Jehovah. (The King James Version of the Bible translates El as God and Jehovah as Lord.) I will just give you a few of my favorites and their meanings here. I encourage you to look up all of His names either in a reference book or on the internet.

Elohim: "Supreme God" or "Mighty God."

It is the first name of God in the Bible in Genesis 1:1: "God created the heavens and the earth." Interestingly enough, it is a plural word in Hebrew, which reflects the triune nature of God.

El Elyon: "The Most High God"

He who dwells in the secret place of the Most High... (Psalm 91:1).

El Shaddai: "God Almighty"

...Shall abide in the shadow of the Almighty (Psalm 91:1).

El Roi: "The God Who Sees"

Then she called the name of the Lord who spoke to her, You-Are-the-God-Who-Sees; for she said, "Have I also here seen Him who sees me?" (Genesis 16:13)

Jehovah Jireh: "The Lord Will Provide"

And Abraham called the name of the place, The-Lord-Will-Provide; as it is said to this day, "In the Mount of the Lord it shall be provided" (Genesis 22:14).

Jehovah Rapha: "The Lord Who Heals You"

If you diligently heed the voice of the Lord your God and do what is right in His sight, give ear to His commandments and keep all His statutes, I will put none of the diseases on you which I have brought on the Egyptians. For I am the Lord who heals you" (Exodus 15:26).

Jehovah Nissi: "The Lord is My Banner"

This is the name of God that proclaims His divine protection, leadership, and deliverance as we are brought together under Him. After Israel defeated Amalek, by the Lord's hand, the Bible records, "Moses built an altar and called its name, The-Lord-Is-My-Banner" (Exod. 17:15).

Jehovah Tsidkenu: "The Lord Our Righteousness"

Now this is His name by which He will be called: the Lord our righteousness (Jeremiah 23:6).

Jehovah M'Kaddesh: "The Lord Who Sanctifies"

He makes us holy (sets us apart unto Himself): "And you shall be holy to Me, for I the Lord am holy, and have separated you from the peoples, that you should be Mine" (Lev. 20:26).

Jehovah Shamma: "The Lord Who Reveals Himself to Us Unceasingly" or "The Lord Who Has Not Abandoned Us"

And the name of the city from that day shall be: the Lord is there (Ezekiel 48:35).

Jehovah Rohi: "The Lord is Our Shepherd"

The Lord is my shepherd. I have all that I need (Psalm 23:1 NLT).

Jehovah Sabaoth: "The Lord of Hosts"

The Lord of the heavenly armies—the angelic hosts. It says in Psalm 34:7, "The angel of the Lord encamps all around those who fear Him, and He delivers them" and also in Psalm 24:10, "Who is this King of glory? The Lord of hosts, he is the King of glory."

Jehovah Shalom: "The Lord is Peace"

I like this definition of the Hebrew word for peace, which is *shalom,* as "nothing lacking, nothing broken." When Gideon saw the Angel of the Lord face to face, the Word says: "Then the Lord said to him, 'Peace be with you; do not fear, you shall not die.' So Gideon built an altar there to the Lord, and called it The-Lord-Is-Peace" (Judg. 6:23-24).

I have heard people say that they cannot praise the Lord in prayer because they run out of things to praise Him for. All we have to do is start blessing His name by recognizing who He is to us and we will never run out of things to praise Him with. Many times I just start going through each of His names one by one and blessing that name for who He is to me in my life.

Let me give you an example of what that might sound like here:

*Lord, I praise You because You are Mighty God.
There is no one like You. You are God Most High
and there is none other. I praise You because You are
El Roi and always see me, have Your eyes of love upon
me, and care for me. I praise You because You are*

Jehovah Jireh, the Lord who provides for me, so I will never have to worry or go without.

You are Jehovah Rapha, the Lord who heals me, and I praise You for that. There are so many times I needed Your healing power in my life and You came through. When people take advantage of me or when the enemy attacks me, You are Jehovah Nisi, my banner and my victory, many times telling me to "stand still and see the great thing I am about to do." I praise You, Lord, that You are Jehovah Tsidkenu, my righteousness, because I'm incapable of standing rightly before You on my own, so You sent Jesus to pay the penalty for my sins. You are Jehovah M'Kaddesh, the One who sanctifies me and makes me holy, set apart unto Yourself that where You are I may be also.

I praise You, Lord, because You are Jehovah Shammah and have never abandoned me. You are always there with me. As You have said that You would never leave me or forsake me, always be with me in trouble, hear my prayers and answer me, and show me Your salvation. I praise You, Lord, because You are Jehovah Rohi, my Shepherd, and Psalm 23 tells me how much You love me and take care of me. You even safely leave the other 99 sheep just to come after me when I wander away.

I praise You, Lord, because You are Jehovah Sabaoth, the Lord of the armies of Heaven, and You encamp Your holy angels about me to keep me from harm.

You have commanded them to minister to me to the point of lifting me up so I wouldn't even strike my foot upon a stone. You protect me and deliver me from harm and I can always trust You.

Finally, Lord, I praise You for being Jehovah Shalom, my peace. When I'm afraid, worried, anxious, sad, depressed, or just not at rest, I can turn myself toward You and trust in You to become my peace—nothing lacking, nothing broken.

I could go on and on (and I normally do), but I think you get the idea. I usually have so many more things that I can praise Him for as I remember each of His names, because I have had so many wonderful experiences with Him. He has shown me how much He cares for me in the meaning of that particular attribute of His glorious character.

I exhort you to memorize His names, if not in the Hebrew at least in your own language. Then when you are praising, tell Him how much you appreciate that part of His character as it applies to you. Remember that He wants to show you His goodness in every aspect of living and that by knowing His names you can also know what He will do in your life.

Come Into His Presence with Singing

When we think of praise and worship, we usually think of singing and playing instruments, and that is another way of expressing it. The psalmist says:

Praise God in His sanctuary; praise Him in His mighty firmament! Praise Him for His mighty acts;

praise Him according to His excellent greatness! Praise Him with the sound of the trumpet; praise Him with the lute and harp! Praise Him with the timbrel and dance; praise Him with stringed instruments and flutes! Praise Him with loud cymbals; praise Him with clashing cymbals! Let everything that has breath praise the Lord (Psalm 150).

In most churches that I have been to, musical praise and worship is usually part of almost every service. People sing, clap, raise their hands, or even move or dance to the music and songs of the worship band. The words to the songs may be in books, song sheets, or projected on the walls so that everyone can join in praise to the Lord. Obviously, this kind of praise doesn't have to be done only in a corporate church setting, but musical praise can happen anywhere, even at home (and it should).

Music has a way of creating an atmosphere that encourages our emotions to embrace the experience. This is a good thing as long as it is genuine praise and not just about expressing those emotions for our own sake. We know the difference by where our focus is. Is it on us, or is it on the Lord? Have you ever sung a song to the Lord and weren't even paying attention to what you were saying? I definitely have, and that isn't praise. True praise is always about exalting the Lord for His goodness. If we are just singing the words because they are a part of the song but not meaning what we are saying, then that isn't praise.

I challenge you. The next time you are going to sing to the Lord, ask the Holy Spirit to make you fully aware of what you are saying and how it applies to your personal relationship with the Father. Then sing like you are singing the words to the Lord

Himself in the secret place you have established with Him. Just like it says, "Come before His Presence with singing." You will never sing that song the same way again. Your praise will be richer and you will experience His Presence in a greater measure.

Worship

Worship is different from praise because it focuses totally on God and not on us at all. We worship God because of His very nature, just because of His greatness. The posture of worship is to be prostrate, bowing so low in adoration that we are on our faces before His throne. An example of worship is found in Revelation 4:

> *The four living creatures, each having six wings, were full of eyes around and within. And they do not rest day or night, saying: "Holy, holy, holy, Lord God Almighty, who was and is and is to come!"*
>
> *Whenever the living creatures give glory and honor and thanks to Him who sits on the throne, who lives forever and ever, the twenty-four elders fall down before Him who sits on the throne and worship Him who lives forever and ever, and cast their crowns before the throne, saying:*
>
> *"You are worthy, O Lord, to receive glory and honor and power; for You created all things, and by Your will they exist and were created"* (Revelation 4:8-11).

I used to wonder how the four living creatures and the 24 elders could do that for all eternity and still have the same wonder and amazement every time they spoke those words. Don't they get bored doing the same thing over and over again? That was my question until one day when I heard Pastor Alex Barefoot speaking on this very subject. He said to picture the scene in Heaven. Here are the creatures and elders before the throne of the infinite and glorious Lord God Almighty. They look up at Him and see one aspect of His nature and are so awestruck with not only what they see, but also what they experience in that moment, that they bow down and worship Him with the only words they can utter.

Holy, holy, holy, Lord God Almighty, who was and is and is to come! You are worthy, O Lord, to receive glory and honor and power; for You created all things, and by Your will they exist and were created.

Then they look up again, and see another aspect of their God that they have never seen before, and gasp in wonder and amazement at His greatness one more time, saying the same words all over again in response to what they have seen and experienced in that moment, because there are no other words that can express it better. And because our God is infinite, this happens over and over again for all eternity. Every time it happens, they see something new, something they have never seen before, and just as great and amazing as anything they have ever experienced.

That explanation helped me so much to understand true worship. It's not about me at all. It is just about Him.

In the book of Daniel, we see three men who understood true worship. They understood that worship belongs only to God and doesn't depend on whether He shows His goodness to them or not.

Shadrach, Meshach and Abednego replied to him, "King Nebuchadnezzar, we do not need to defend ourselves before you in this matter. If we are thrown into the blazing furnace, the God we serve is able to deliver us from it, and he will deliver us from Your Majesty's hand. But even if he does not, we want you to know, Your Majesty, that we will not serve your gods or worship the image of gold you have set up" (Daniel 3:16-18 NIV).

When we get to this point of true worship as we are coming into His Presence, we are in the correct posture of humility and amazement before our God. We understand more fully who He is and the greatness of what He has done for us. We also understand our place in our relationship with our Lord and are ready to have communion with Him.

Prayer

Prayer is simply defined as communication with God. We need to always remember that in communication, the conversation goes both ways. We listen as well as speak. Communication is both verbal and non-verbal. Words aren't always necessary or even preferable. Thanksgiving, praise, blessing, and worship are all part of prayer, but they are really only one side of the conversation. Once we are in His Presence, with the right attitude, we always need to be listening for anything the Lord wants to communicate back to us.

This information may come in many forms. He can speak through His Word. He can speak through a still small voice or an impression to our heart or mind. He may speak through a pastor, a family member, or a friend. He might use a prophetic word from someone or a song, television program, or movie. He can give you a vision or a dream. And yes, He can use someone you don't even like. Never limit God's creativeness when it comes to Him communicating His love to us.

One place many people struggle is asking God questions. They think, "He's God, if He wants me to know something, then He will tell me." But God wants us to ask Him things.

Ask and it will be given to you; seek and you will find; knock and the door will be opened to you. For everyone who asks receives; the one who seeks finds; and to the one who knocks, the door will be opened (Matthew 7:7-8 NIV).

If any of you lacks wisdom, you should ask God, who gives generously to all without finding fault, and it will be given to you (James 1:5 NIV).

He delights in showing us His great wisdom. He has the right answers to all of life's questions. If we don't ask, then we just assume that if He doesn't provide the information we need, we are just supposed to take the matter into our own hands. Most of the time this leads to a situation that isn't His will for us, because we are leaning on our own worldly wisdom rather than His divine wisdom.

I find that my best times of communion with the Lord are when I come in desperation for Him. In those times I realize my own inadequacies in dealing with life and remove all of my expectations about how He might answer me or help me resolve the situations I am in. He loves to amaze me with His mercy, grace, and goodness. He answers me in ways that cause me to thank, praise, bless, and worship Him with great joy.

"For my thoughts are not your thoughts, neither are your ways my ways," declares the Lord. *"As the heavens are higher than the earth, so are my ways higher than your ways and my thoughts than your thoughts"* (Isaiah 55:8-9 NIV).

One of the questions I'm asking more and more of the Holy Spirit is why I do some of the things I do, especially when I know that they aren't what Jesus would do. I turn to the Holy Spirit, point at myself as though I'm on the outside looking in, and ask Him, "Now why did I just say that?" or "Why did I do that instead of what I should have done?" Then I just get quiet and wait for the answer. His insights are amazing because He knows me much better than I do, and those insights help me to repent so I have less of a tendency to say or do it that way again.

I believe that the ultimate place we want with the Lord is to just be in His Presence without saying anything at all, to spend time enjoying Him as our "Abba." The Aramaic word *Abba* means Father, but in a deeply personal and intimate way. It is an endearing term given only to the Person we feel is the One who loves us like no one else can or does. This place we are talking about is that secret place spoken of in Psalm 91. It is a place of safety where we are totally at rest in the Presence of our Abba. We know that if we have a need He will take care of it. If we have a tear, He will dry it. If we aren't able to be at rest, He will give us His peace. It is a place where we are overwhelmed by His love and His goodness. A place where we feel we are truly home.

Staying in His Presence

Once we get into our secret place with Him, we never want to leave. Unfortunately, for most of us, our old habits take hold and we are thrust back into our daily grind. The cares and duties of life seem to take over. We may become disillusioned and feel that staying in that place is impossible. If that is so, then why did the Lord say, "He who dwells in the secret place abides under the shadow of the Almighty" in the first verse of Psalm 91? If He said we can make our home there, it must be possible. I'm not saying that I have attained that constancy, but the Lord is teaching me how to stay there longer and longer even in the face of living in a temporal world.

If I wander away from that place, it helps me to return when I go back through what got me there before: thanksgiving, praise, blessing, singing, worship, and prayer. As I realign my posture, I realize how much I miss His Presence and I want to stay there forever. I'm learning that the more time I set aside to be in that place with Him, the easier it is to stay there even in the journey of life. I interact more with Him during the day as I know He is right there with me, wanting to help me to be victorious over the enemy and to be conformed into the image of His Son Jesus.

Before I try to do life my own way, I ask for His wisdom and His way of doing things. Then He answers me and my perspective of other people changes when I realize that we are all God's children and that most of us are trying to do life in our own strength. I remember that we are all God's favorites and that it is my assignment here on the earth to love His children. He wants me to accomplish that by praying for them and re-presenting Jesus to them so they can be reconciled back to the Father who loves them as much as He loves me. He reminds me that He has a destiny and a purpose for their life too, if they could just get to know Him. He makes it very clear to me that a big part of my destiny is to introduce them to Him.

I agree with the apostle Paul when he said:

> *Not that I have already obtained all this, or have already arrived at my goal, but I press on to take hold of that for which Christ Jesus took hold of me. Brothers and sisters, I do not consider myself yet to have taken hold of it. But one thing I do: Forgetting what is behind and straining toward what is ahead, I press on toward the goal to win the prize for which God has called me heavenward in Christ Jesus* (Philippians 3:12-14 NIV).

Roberts Lairdon, in his book *God's Generals*, quotes John G. Lake as saying, "It became easy for me to detach myself from the course of life, so that while my hands and mind were engaged in the common affairs of everyday life, my spirit maintained its attitude of communion with God."

This gives me great hope that this is possible. If he was able to do this, then we can too. We can live in this world, but not be like the people of this world. We can dwell in the secret place with His Presence continually and still have our hands and minds be engaged in the common affairs of everyday life.

So I exhort you to press ever forward to that goal that God destined you to obtain, that you would be conformed into the image of Jesus who was always in the Presence of the Father.

As Jesus prayed:

*And the glory which You gave Me I have given them,
that they may be one just as We are one: I in them,
and You in Me; that they may be made perfect in
one, and that the world may know that You have
sent Me, and have loved them as You have loved Me*
(John 17:22-23).

Chapter 13

CALLED OUT

JOE

God was gracious in sending us to Impact. We had learned so much there under the ministry of Pastors Donna and Terry Wise. I remember when we first started attending the church we saw it as both a hospital and a university for us. It wasn't only the place and people that God used to walk us through my healing, but a school where we were exposed to principles of the Kingdom that we had never heard before. Many guest speakers came and shared what was going on in ministry all over the world. There were apostles, prophets, evangelists, pastors, and teachers who were equipping us to do the work of ministry. At this time we were very involved at Impact.

I was helping in the audiovisual department and Heidi was the lead pianist in the worship band. Little did we suspect, but after six and a half years of schooling God decided it was time that we graduate and be released and called us out to another place to put into practice what we had learned.

We had some friends who knew that Heidi and I love music and especially love worshiping the Lord. They invited us to a little church for a Wednesday night worship service because they wanted us to hear the really good worship band there. I told them that I rarely ever go to other churches for services and am very loyal to my own church. They said that even though they used to go to this church, they were not currently attending there. They reassured us that they weren't trying to get us to go there permanently, but for just one service. Impact didn't, at that time, have a Wednesday night service, so I reluctantly agreed.

Eastside Church was only about a mile from our home. We have lived in our current house for over 20 years and I passed that church almost every day going to work. I wondered sometimes about what kind of church it was, but I never had a good reason to go in to find out.

We walked into the sanctuary, with our friends who had invited us there, just before the service started. A few people, who knew our friends, introduced themselves. But before we had a chance to meet the pastor, the worship service began. The music was really wonderful and you could feel the Presence of the Lord in the room. As I was really enjoying worshiping the Lord, He spoke to me. His voice wasn't audible, but it was so loud in my spirit that I felt like it was. That voice was from the same God who told me to marry Heidi, the same Lord who spoke to me in the vision I had about our first son, and the same Father who told me ILUVUJOE. I knew it was Him.

"I want you to come to this church and serve this pastor," the Lord said. I felt an implied, "Will you do this?" even though it wasn't said. Because I knew it was His voice, my spirit leaped up within me and I said, "Yes" even before I had a chance to think out what that would mean. Now I'm not one to jump at anything. I'm a person that doesn't like change. "For how long do You want me to do that, Lord?" I asked. "For a season," He said. "How long is that?" I asked. "I'm not going to tell you that yet," He replied.

I made an appointment with Alex Barefoot, the lead pastor of Eastside Church. I didn't even know what he or the church believed. I wanted to sit down and understand this man the Lord told me to serve. We didn't agree on everything, few people do, but I had an immediate love for him as a brother and I admired his passion and dedication to the Lord and His work. I told Pastor Alex what the Lord had spoken to me. I interpreted the word serve to mean to help him, pray for him, encourage him, and exhort him. The Lord also warned me to do exactly what He had spoken to me and to especially not seek any positions of leadership at Eastside. I was there as a servant.

I knew I had to be obedient to the Lord. I told Pastors Donna and Terry what had happened and they were gracious to release me for however long the Lord needed me. That next Sunday I was part of the congregation of Eastside Church.

HEIDI

Joe told me what the Lord had spoken to him that evening. I really didn't know what to make of it. The Lord had asked Joe, but He hadn't mentioned what I was supposed to do. I was very involved at Impact and felt like that was where I was supposed to stay at that time. Besides, the Lord hadn't told Joe how long he was going to be at Eastside. We had always gone to the same church, but Joe said I should stay at Impact if that is what the Lord was telling me. He just knew he had to be obedient to what God had asked of him. I thought he would "get it out of his system" in a month or so. Joe never pressured me to leave Impact. He did ask that I would come to Eastside for a few events and some Wednesday night services when I could. He missed worshiping together as much as I did.

We attended a newcomers dinner at Eastside together. After the dinner, each of the pastors and leaders of the church told something about themselves and their history at Eastside. One particular thing impressed me. It was the passion of the young leadership there. Even though Pastor Alex was near our age, he had amassed a group of leaders who were much younger. They were in their 20s and 30s. The church itself was full of young people. They had been praying to the Lord to send older, more mature Christians to help mentor the young people of the church. God was answering those prayers and we heard stories from many people about how God brought them, in His mysterious ways, to the church.

JOE

After that meeting I was talking to a person whom we knew from Impact but who lives near us. She had never gone to Eastside and knew nothing about it, although, like us, had passed it often. One day when she and her husband were driving by Eastside, the Lord spoke to her. "There are young people in that church who are praying for Me to send them mature mentors."

The effective, fervent prayer of a righteous man avails much (James 5:16).

I began to pray for Pastor Alex almost every day. He usually is the first person in my prayer times. I pray for the Lord to bless him with wisdom on how to lead; for health and strength in his physical body; for dreams, visions, words of knowledge, and prophecies from the Spirit; and for finances to meet his every need. I also pray for the people of the church, especially those who are designated as leaders and those who don't have a title but are leading by example. I pray for the church to become a lighthouse in the city, state, nation, and the world. I also pray that God will bring provision and all the resources that the church will need to achieve its destiny.

God was giving me a love not only for Pastor Alex but also the leaders and people of Eastside Church. I began loving on them, asking them about themselves and finding out what they needed from the Lord. As I did this I was able to pray more specific prayers for them and encourage them to seek the Lord for their requests because He wanted to answer them. I would tell them that each one of them is God's favorite, because God had revealed that to me.

One of my best analogies for how much He loves us came from being a young father to my first son. Sometimes I would watch him sleeping in his crib, just waiting for him to wake up. When he opened his eyes I would get so excited and say something like, "Hey Joey, good morning, so what are we going to do today together?" To me that's how I view the way the Father sees each one of us. Again, like the Lord showed me, because He is infinite He has infinite love, time, resources, mercy, grace, and patience for each of His children. He treats every one of us like we are the only child He has.

It had been a few months since the Lord had called me to Eastside and I began seeing people healed and lives being restored in the church. I started to realize that the reason the Lord had sent me there wasn't only for me to minister, but also that the Lord was beginning a new phase of D.E.A.R. in my life. I was learning by serving and being obedient to His call. Heidi was still quite involved at Impact Church in the music ministry, and I didn't like that we were going to two different churches, so I again began to ask the Lord how long the "season" at Eastside was going to be. "Settle in, you will be there for a while," He answered. "Okay, Lord," I said. Now I just needed to tell Heidi.

HEIDI

I really thought that Joe was only going to be at Eastside for a couple of months at best. I told him that I felt like I should continue ministering on the worship team at Impact until the Lord allowed him to return. What I didn't tell him was that the Lord had started dealing with my heart also. He started telling me that my time at Impact was coming to an end and I was to join Joe at Eastside. He said that Joe and I needed to serve together and that I needed to spend more time with my grandchildren. I also noticed that my passion had begun to wane in "leading" worship and it was no longer going to be at the forefront where it had been for the last two to three decades.

I, like Joe, am a very loyal person. I felt if I left now, I would really hurt the worship ministry at Impact and I grieved over that. While I continued to be loyal at Impact, the Lord started to ask me when I was going to be obedient and answer His call. I realize now that it was an unrecognized "trust" issue in my life. I had become very comfortable there and was afraid to venture into the unknown.

When Joe finally informed me that God had told him that he would be there for a while, it confirmed what the Lord was saying to me. I was very reluctant, but I decided I had to be obedient. I informed Pastors Donna and Terry what the Lord had told me, received their blessing, and started attending Eastside with Joe. The Lord was about to teach both of us more about ourselves, what it really means to be a servant, and the blessings that true obedience brings.

Chapter 14

THE POWER OF TESTIMONY

JOE

We knew testimonies were powerful faith builders, but we didn't know how prolific they really could be. This was a lesson we were about to learn. We see in the New Testament how testimonies of healing brought people from all around to Jesus and they were healed. After the woman with the issue of blood was healed by touching the hem of His garment, they would lay people in the streets in the path of Jesus so that they could touch His hem and be healed. The testimonies of the miracles performed by Peter were so prevalent that they would lay people in the streets so that his shadow would pass over them and they were healed. The testimonies of miracles performed by Paul were so powerful that they would only have to take cloths from his body to the sick and they would be healed.

I knew what testimonies did for me. Every time I would see or hear about someone being healed, especially from something similar to what I was suffering with, my faith would rise up and say, "Maybe that was real. Maybe I can be healed too!"

Without testimonies, I don't believe I would be alive today. As I have related the testimonies of what God has done for me, I have watched people's faces light up in faith, and have even seen them healed as they believed healing was theirs also. I personally try to always tell people a testimony of an answer to prayer for a situation related to theirs before I pray for them.

A minister once told me, "If you don't have your own testimony, pull on someone else's testimony until God gives you your own." So, if I don't have a testimony of my own of God meeting a person's need in a certain area, I use one from someone else who is reliable that I know. A testimony says if the Lord has done it for one person, then He is willing to do it again for you. It creates an atmosphere of faith where God can move mightily.

Let me give you an example of how testimonies are prolific as they build on each other.

One day Eric, a brother in the Lord, and I were putting up signs in front of Eastside Church. He was up on a ladder and hitting a piece of wood with a sledgehammer to pound sign posts into the hard North Carolina red clay. After he had been doing that for quite a while, he stopped and began to try to zip-tie a sign onto the posts. All of a sudden, he grabbed his finger and cried out, "Man that really hurts." The trauma of the sledgehammer hitting the wood had caused incredible nerve pain in that finger. Without so much as a thought I said, "Give me that finger," and I grabbed it in my hand as he held it down to me. "Finger, you be healed right now in the name of Jesus. We don't have time for this. We are trying to do some work for the Lord here. Nerve pain, go! Inflammation, go! Be restored in the name of Jesus!" I said in a normal, but authoritative voice.

As I let go of his finger, he said, "Thank you." When he began to reach back up to the sign he stopped, stared wide-eyed at his finger, and said in an amazed voice, "It's gone. The pain is gone!" I was almost as surprised as he was and we both rejoiced as we finished the work.

A few days later I was paying for groceries and talking to the lady cashier. It was very interesting because even though the store was busy, no one was in line behind me. (The Lord does this a lot for me when He wants to give me time to minister to someone.) As I began to tell her about Eric's finger healing, and a little about my own testimony, I noticed that the person who was bagging for me was listening intently too. The cashier looked at me and said, "That is amazing. Will you pray for my husband?" "What is wrong with him?" I inquired. "He has cancer," she answered. "I will do better than that. Are you a Christian?" I asked. She was, so I continued, "I'm going to pray over your hands. After I do that I want you to lay your hands on your husband every chance you get and tell that cancer to go in the name of Jesus. It doesn't belong there and you have the authority to command it to go as a child of God."

I prayed for her hands right there at the counter. I had no sooner finished praying when people started coming into her line.

When I saw her a month later I asked, "Are you doing what I asked you to do?" "Yes, I most certainly am," she replied. "How is he doing?" I questioned. "He's quite well. He's out fishing today!" she said with a smile on her face. About a month later, I saw her again at the store. "How's your husband doing now?" I asked. She smiled even bigger than the last time. "He is cancer-free!" she exclaimed.

I was sharing these testimonies with my church family also. One night after service, Kristen, the wife of one of the men in the church, was telling me how every time her husband went out of town on business he told her to be careful while he was away. He had told me before in other conversations that she was accident prone. I went out to their car and said, "Instead of saying those kinds of things about your wife, you should speak blessing over her and your family and pray for her while you are away." About two days later he texted me and told me he needed to tell me a testimony.

"My wife has been dealing with severe shoulder pain for almost a year now," he said. "She couldn't even raise her arm above her head and definitely couldn't lift up anything heavy at all," he continued. "Today I laid my hand on her and prayed a simple prayer of healing for her shoulder. I went into my home office and very shortly after that I heard her calling to me. As I looked into the kitchen to find her I could see that she was holding one of our children in the arm with the good shoulder and was waving the other arm around. 'Look honey,' she said, 'No pain. And look what else I can do.' She took some heavy bowls, lifted them above her head and placed them into the cabinet," he said excitedly. To this day she hasn't had that shoulder issue again.

HEIDI

When we went down to Texas for some ministry classes, we met many other students from all over the world. We made sure that each one we met knew of Joe's healing and we also encouraged them with these more recent testimonies too. As we were sharing, one lady said that she had the same issue with her shoulder that the woman at our church had. She asked if we would pray for it. Because Joe tries to activate people in healing, he turned to her husband and said, "You lay your hand on her shoulder and pray and we will lay our hands on yours and agree." After the man prayed, his wife moved her shoulder around into different positions and declared that the pain was gone. She said it was still a little sore, but we had been taught by Joan Hunter that when the pain is gone, the soreness sometimes just needs to be "worked out" as things get back to normal.

Later the same day we were in line to pick up some materials for our class. We were telling the lady in front of us these testimonies. She said before she came for ordination she was moving some racks of clothing in her store and had hurt her arm. It was in pain at that very moment. We offered to pray for her right there. After we prayed we asked how her arm was feeling. She said it was still painful, but we encouraged her to keep speaking to her arm and telling it to line up with the Word of the Lord. About 30 minutes later we were all in a service worshiping together. This lady was about 15 feet from us. All of a sudden she turned to us and gave us a "thumbs up." The pain was gone. She had been healed. Hallelujah!

This is an example of the power of testimonies. This powerful line of testimonies lives on as we hear reports of people continuing to be healed as they realize, through these stories, that God is still healing through His people today and that He wants to heal them. The important thing to note is that a testimony, even if it isn't your own, can activate faith in both you and the person you are praying for. It also becomes something you can go back to and reflect on when the enemy tries to bring doubt or when you go through a time when healing seems elusive.

I want to relate one more story that exemplifies another healing principle. Anita, a lady in our church, had terrible, debilitating pain in her elbow because of a detached tendon. She had two surgeries to reattach it, but it would inflame and detach again. After her third surgery she was still in a tremendous amount of pain and had limited range of motion. The doctor said it looked like the tendon was getting ready to detach again. She sent an email to the church that things were not right with her arm and that the pain was off the charts and asked for prayer. I was very upset because we and others had prayed for her many times with seemingly no results.

I knew that I would see her that night and wanted to encourage her and pray for her again. I saw her about four minutes before the service began and I said, "I'm mad!" She knew I was talking about the fact that she was still dealing with pain and replied, "Me too!" I told her the devil is a liar and that it is God's will for her to be healed. "It's not a matter of if you are going to be healed, but only when," I declared. I wanted to pray for her right then, but the service was starting.

During worship, Christine, one of our worship leaders, stopped playing the piano and in tears told the congregation that she wasn't supposed to sing the song she was scheduled for that night. The

Lord was present and it was a powerful moment as she related that He was teaching her a lesson about her attitude toward worship and felt that one of the other singers should just do the next song. When the worship concluded, Christine sat down beside Anita. At the end of the service Pastor Alex had the congregation stand and hold hands for a closing prayer. Anita tried to keep anyone from touching her arm but Christine grabbed her hand anyway.

As soon as she touched Anita's hand, they both felt something. Christine said she could feel the power of the Holy Spirit "release" from her and Anita described it as something like a lightning bolt surge through her arm. They looked at each other in surprise and Christine exclaimed, "Did you feel that?" Anita replied excitedly, "How could I not?" At that moment Anita realized the pain was totally gone and it has never come back! They weren't even praying for healing, but she was healed anyway. Anita says that she wasn't even mentally "there" for the service or even thinking about healing, but she was healed anyway. Christine told us, "Afterward, I thanked God for healing Anita and couldn't help but feel that God can use anyone, at any time, for any reason He chooses."

Yes, many times God heals just because He can. He heals us because He loves us and it is His desire that we be whole. I believe He let Christine be a part of the miracle because of her passion for the Lord and her obedience and humility in the worship service.

This incident also created line of testimonies of healing. A few weeks later Christine saw Andrew limping in the parking lot. "What is wrong with your foot?" she asked. "Oh, it has been hurting me for a while," he said. Many of us had prayed for Andrew's foot, but it hadn't been healed. "Let me pray for it," Christine said. After she prayed, Andrew no longer limped. The pain was gone.

On another Sunday, Andrew came up to us so that we could pray for his shoulder that was in pain. Heidi and I prayed for him and encouraged him to speak to his shoulder and tell it to line up with the Word of God. That week while he was washing dishes, that shoulder was giving him pain again. He stopped and told his shoulder, "Shoulder, you don't control me, I control you. In the name of Jesus I command the pain to stop!" The pain stopped. Five minutes later, the pain started again and he said, "No, I'm in control of you. Stop in the name of Jesus!" It stopped again. He did that five more times and then the pain left completely.

Andrew does lawn care as a side job. One day as he was finishing up a job, he began having severe back pain. He could barely get in his truck and drive home. That night, as he was tucking his two-year-old son Micah into bed, he grimaced in pain as he stood up from kneeling in prayer at the bedside. "What's wrong, Daddy?" Micah asked. Andrew told him that he had hurt his back while working that day. "Jesus, Daddy's back. Amen," Micah prayed. Immediately the pain in Andrew's back was gone and he told Micah that God had answered his prayer for his daddy.

Andrew says that whenever any of them isn't feeling well, Micah will pray for them with authority and conviction and he sounds like a little Dr. Joe. Actually, he sounds like his dad who testifies to Micah of the power of prayer and demonstrates that to his son, who in turn demonstrates it to others.

Testimonies are powerful. They create a culture of faith for miracles, healing, and restoration. In that atmosphere people really believe they can heal and be healed. But there is also one more giant benefit of the power of testimony. It makes witnessing easy.

Chapter 15

YOU SHALL BE WITNESSES

JOE

I remember one Christian teacher talking about evangelism. "Some win the lost at any cost. I teach the found while they're still around," he said. He was a teacher and I believe that he felt witnessing to strangers was hard, but the Lord had given him a teaching gift, so he felt he could just ignore the evangelism part. I now know this isn't correct theology. Witnessing isn't only a vital part of the Christian life; it's a command from the Lord.

And He said to them, "Go into all the world and preach the gospel to every creature" (Mark 16:15).

Legally and biblically, a witness is someone who has personally seen, heard, or experienced something. In the courtroom, a judge isn't interested in what the witness might have read or heard secondhand as hearsay. He wants to know what they have experienced firsthand; otherwise, they aren't considered a credible witness, and he will tell the jury to disregard their testimony. In some churches witnessing has been defined as telling people what the Bible says and not about personal experiences with the power of God that line up with His Word.

When Peter and John were told to stop speaking about Jesus, this is what happened:

> *So they called them and commanded them not to speak at all nor teach in the name of Jesus. But Peter and John answered and said to them, "Whether it is right in the sight of God to listen to you more than to God, you judge. For we cannot but speak the things which we have seen and heard"* (Acts 4:18-20).

They had *"seen* and *heard!"* They had witnessed something and they couldn't help themselves. They had experienced God and everyone had to know. John puts it this way:

> *That which was from the beginning, which we have heard, which we have seen with our eyes, which we have looked upon, and our hands have handled, concerning the Word of life—the life was manifested, and we have seen, and bear witness, and declare to you that eternal life which was with the Father and was manifested to us—that which we have seen and heard we declare to you, that you also may have*

*fellowship with us; and truly our fellowship is with
the Father and with His Son Jesus Christ. And these
things we write to you that your joy may be full*
(1 John 1:1-4).

They had seen Jesus. They had heard Him and touched Him.
They had experienced the Messiah, the Son of God, who brought
them eternal life. They were compelled as witnesses of this amazing truth to tell everyone, so they could experience Him too. This
is what being a true witness is.

Before I understood this, witnessing was hard for me. One reason was that I had a misconception of what witnessing really was
all about. For me, witnessing was picking out a neighborhood and
going door to door with a Bible in hand telling them what it said
about the Lord and trying to get them saved. I could talk to people about God if they were already Christians, or those people I
knew very well, but not complete strangers. I felt like I was bother-
ing them or getting into their personal space.

That all changed when I realized it wasn't just about what the
Bible said or what someone else told me. I had my own testimonies.
I would tell anyone and everyone who would listen. It didn't matter to me if they were Christians or not. I could witness to them
because I had experienced things that the Lord had done in my
own life that were so wonderful, everyone would want to hear.

If they just knew how awesome God is and what He has done
for us, then they would want to know Him too. If I told them
that they too were His favorite children and He wants to bless
them like He blesses me, they would be so excited. I wasn't both-
ering them. I was informing them about something I knew about

from firsthand experience. It wasn't like I had to tell them so I got Christian brownie points or something. They just needed to know.

Jesus never said to just be a witness to the lost. In fact, He sent the disciples to the cities and towns of Israel, who were already called the chosen children of God. They were to tell them the good news of His Kingdom that was now among them.

If we only target the unsaved, we miss a tremendous mission field. Currently polls say that eight out of ten people in the United States claim to be Christians. If we are just looking for the lost to tell them about the goodness of the Lord, that severely limits us. We are supposed to be witnesses to everyone we come in contact with. They all need to hear that Jesus is alive and well and who God says He is and that the Kingdom is here because of Him. He told us to demonstrate the good news of His Kingdom through healing the sick, raising the dead, casting out devils, and cleansing lepers in His name. It is the goodness and kindness of God that leads people, both saved and unsaved, to repentance.

That realization changed the way I approach witnessing. I used to ask people if they were Christians, or knew Jesus, or at least if they went to church before I would decide if I should talk to them about the Lord. If we are supposed to be witnessing to everyone, that question is irrelevant. All it does is to set the stage for judgment, intimidation, or offense, and we don't need to hinder the good news with those filters on either side of the conversation. When I meet someone, I just testify to them about what God is doing. I tell them about the things I have witnessed. To this point, I have never had anyone turn me down. They want to hear the stories of His mercy, kindness, goodness, and grace and the fact that He wants them to enjoy His blessings too as they get to know Him.

I make sure that the people closest to me know my testimonies. I tell my family, my friends, my co-workers, and especially my brothers and sisters at church about them. I tell my testimonies to the cashiers and workers at the store. I tell them to people I meet when I'm out walking, exercising, shopping, banking, or when I go to a restaurant. When anyone asks me how I'm doing, my normal reply is, "I'm blessed and highly favored," which elicits many different, but usually positive, responses. And I make sure I tell everyone to be blessed as a parting word. If given the chance, I pray for their needs, and many times we see the answers to those prayers. If they don't express a need, I ask them if I can just pray a blessing over them

My testimonies usually bring a smile to a face or a look of amazement. When I tell them the story of "ILUVUJOE" it brings tears to the eyes of many and a new hope that God loves them specially too. If I ask someone if I can pray for them, very few ever say no. Most are appreciative that you care about them. Many are amazed that you're going to pray for them right then and there. I try to treat people like Jesus would treat them. I try to be kind and caring. I give them a smile and always give them my full attention. Remember, the way many Christians have presented Christ in the past has given Him a bad rap. It is my responsibility to re-present Jesus to them. The Holy Spirit in us will do that if we will just let Him. This is what witnessing is all about.

HEIDI

We were in a home-improvement store buying some items for our house. We stopped to talk to a store salesperson and started to tell him the story of Joe's healing. He was amazed, so we began telling him many of the other testimonies of people being healed and restored as we had prayed for them over the past several years. He listened for over 30 minutes hanging on every word about the goodness of God. At the end of the conversation, he said, "You know, I'm not the religious person in our family, my wife is, but after talking to you both, I'm seriously considering going back to church." He just needed someone to show him the reality of the Gospel. As we have said before, when we testify of the goodness and kindness of God, it leads people to the place of repentance.

Another day, at the same store, I was looking for a toilet flapper. I couldn't find the particular one for our brand of toilet, so I asked one of the employees there to help me. I thought I was only going to be there a few minutes, but because that wasn't this man's department, it turned into over a half an hour of looking. I finally just picked out three flappers to take home hoping one of them would work. I thanked the man, and was just about to leave, when the the Holy Spirit said, "You're missing a chance to minister here." I had noticed that the man was wearing a veteran's cap, so I turned back to him and said, "Sir, are you a veteran?" He replied that he was, so I said, "Thank you, sir, for your service. It is because of men like you that we are free today. You've had to sacrifice a lot and experienced things you shouldn't have had to experience." "That's true," he said, "and I lost my wife 3 months ago." "I am so very sorry to hear that. Can I pray for you?" I replied. He said, "Yes," so I proceeded to pray a prayer of healing and blessing over him. I prayed that the Holy Spirit would comfort him and be with him and that he would experience God's love for him like never before.

When I was finished, he said with tears in his eyes, "Thank you, ma'am, you have made my day."

Another time at that same store, I met a man in the blinds aisle. He was very friendly and we started a lively conversation. When Joe finally showed up, he was well into his story about what he did for a living. It was a very dangerous line of work. Joe and I were hoping to get in and out of there quickly, but we have learned that we need to listen to the Holy Spirit, because most times when we are inconvenienced, God is up to something. As the conversation stopped, and we were just about to part ways, Joe asked if we could pray for him. He said, "Yes," and we both laid our hands on him to pray. (Yes, right there in the store in front of God and everybody.) We prayed a prayer of protection over him, because of the kind of work he faced every day, and he was very appreciative. Just then I looked at him and said, "Do you have any pain in your body anywhere?" He was a very athletic-looking person, and didn't give any indication that he was in pain, but the Holy Spirit had me ask him that question.

With a surprised look, he told us that he had fallen two stories onto his left shoulder, and it was in pain. He couldn't lift his arm any higher than 45 degrees from the side of his body without it "catching." We asked him if his other shoulder was okay. He readily raised his right arm above his head and said, "That one's fine." Joe asked if we could pray for his painful shoulder, and after a resounding, "Yes," we laid our hands on him and commanded it to be healed in the name of Jesus. We paused and asked him to try it out. He lifted his arm up level with his shoulder. "That feels much better," he said with an amazed look on his face.

"Is that as far as you can lift it?" Joe asked. The man said he thought lifting his arm that far was wonderful enough, but we weren't going to settle for that. So, we laid our hands on him again and prayed a second time. "Now try it," Joe said. The man proceeded to lift his arm straight over his head toward the ceiling. With eyes like saucers he exclaimed, "What did you do? All the pain is gone and it doesn't catch anymore." He continued lifting his arm above his head and dropping it to his side in utter amazement.

As we walked to the front of the store, the man just kept lifting his arm up and down to make sure he was totally whole. When we checked out, Joe asked the man to tell the cashier what had happened. He excitedly said to her, "I couldn't lift my arm any further than this," as he lifted his arm to 45 degrees, "and Mr. Joe prayed for me, and now I can do this," lifting his arm to the sky. As we left the store we could hear the man rejoicing over the goodness God had extended to him that day.

JOE

So, I encourage you to ask the Lord to give you opportunities every day to be His witnesses. There are so many people who are just waiting for someone to demonstrate the Kingdom of God and His love to them. Will you be willing to get out of your comfort zone and share the good news of Jesus? I guarantee, if you start, your joy will be so full that you will never ever be the same again.

The fruit of the righteous is a tree of life, and he who wins souls is wise (Proverbs 11:30).

Chapter 16

ORDAINED

HEIDI

Joan had been asking us to become ordained through her ministry. She knew we had a powerful testimony and felt like we had a call on our lives in the area of healing. She had also been encouraging us to write a book about what we had learned to help others. We appreciated her belief in us, but we weren't sure what God had in store. Every time we would assist her either at her healing schools or just praying for people at the *It's Supernatural!* show tapings, we enjoyed ministering to people and seeing them healed and restored physically, mentally, emotionally, spiritually, and financially. We had done a lot of the preparation for ordination, but didn't feel the urgency.

One day we received another letter in the mail informing us about the opportunity to become ordained through Joan Hunter Ministries (JHM). The date for the ordination was about a month away. Joe was showing it to me when he felt the Lord say to him, "Now is the time." And that's all He said. He didn't give an explanation as to why or what He was going to do with us. Just, "Now is the time." I was surprised, but I have always trusted that when Joe says he has heard the Lord, he has.

JOE

I knew that voice and I knew it was God. The timing wasn't convenient, but many things the Lord asks of us don't come at convenient times. There were a lot of details to handle. We only had two days to the deadline of getting our paperwork in. Some of it involved getting letters of recommendation from our pastors and those who knew us well. We had to get plane tickets and hotel reservations. Most of all, there were prerequisites that we had to finish. We had read most of the books and watched the teaching videos, but it had been a long time. We wanted to study them all over again to make sure we knew the material. Fortunately, we had scheduled a ten-day vacation at the beach that would end ten days before we had to leave for Texas. Most of that vacation time was used finishing the prerequisites before we left for the final ordination classes.

If we had waited even another day it might have been too late to get everything together. It all worked out by the grace of God and we were on a flight to Texas to go to the final classes and become ordained ministers through JHM. Even though we had been to so many different events with Joan, this one was exceptional. We were now making our calling public. During our time there we witnessed many amazing miracles and healings as people prayed.

The atmosphere was electric with faith when we walked into the JHM facility. There were a lot of people in their large meeting room. Some were those who were going to be ordained, some who had already been ordained, and some were JHM staff and volunteers. Most of them were women, and that was great, but I wanted at least one other man I could connect with. I asked the Lord, "You brought me down here for Your purposes. Please let me find a brother in the Lord You want me to bond with." At that moment I saw a tall man standing in the crowd of people in the worship service. I felt the Spirit say, "Him." That evening when Heidi and I were coming back from our hotel, I spotted the same man in the parking lot getting something out of his car. I walked over and introduced myself. His name was Jeff and his wife's name was Kim. It was a divine connection for both Heidi and I, and we had a great time as they were both becoming ordained too.

As I said at the beginning, it was Jeff who not only encouraged me to write this book but had the experience and know-how to help me get it into print. I believe if God gives us a dream, He will also give us the resources we need to see it come to fruition. I know now that one of reasons the Lord told me, "Now is the time," is that He knew Jeff and Kim were going to be there and He created this divine appointment.

It is my prayer that this book has been a divine appointment for you and that you will see that you are God's favorite and that

He has a unique destiny just for you. He has placed you in this world exactly at this time and place because He has Kingdom assignments that only you can accomplish. There is nothing that can stand in your way if you pursue Him with all of your heart, soul, mind, and strength. He is just waiting for you to recognize it and to step into His divine plan for you.

Chapter 17

AND THE JOURNEY CONTINUES

The story of our journey is still not finished. We continue to see signs, miracles, and healings. Every day the Lord teaches us new principles that we didn't know or had ignored in the past. Our pursuit of His Presence gets stronger as time goes on. We have learned to "seek His face and not His hands." Our mission has become clearer and our faith becomes surer. As we share our testimonies, people are being encouraged and are responding to the Lord. This is a sure thing: "A man with an experience is not at the mercy of a man with an argument." People are being released from the chains of the enemy. The fear, lies, and insecurity that shackled them are falling off. The truth is setting them free.

We only wish we had learned these things earlier in life, but we are encouraged that it is still not too late. The Lord told the Messiah in Psalm 2:8, "Ask of Me, and I will give You the nations for Your inheritance, and the ends of the earth for Your possession." We are determined to make an impact on nations for Him.

Will you join us, and those who came before us, and those who will come after us, in taking up that call? We hope that this book, this testimony of the journey to healing and beyond, will help you along on your way to achieve the destiny that the Lord envisioned for you before the beginning of the world.

If you are reading this book and haven't made a decision to make Jesus Christ the Lord of your life, or have drifted away from Him and need to recommit your life to Him, then I ask you to consider doing that right now. You don't have to be sitting in a church or have someone pray for you. Just say something like:

> *Jesus, I have been living life my own way. I haven't been fulfilled doing that. I recognize that I need a relationship with You as Lord over my life. I realize that I have done wrong things against You, myself, and others, and that makes me a sinner and separated from You. I'm asking You to be my Savior and my Lord and to forgive me of all my sins. I thank You for dying on the cross for me and giving me a new life. I commit to reading Your Word and communicating with You every day in prayer. From now on I'm Yours. Thank You, Jesus!*

If you have made a commitment to the Lord just now, please email us at info@encouragingpeople.com and let us know. We want to rejoice with you. Find a church to attend that believes the full gospel and be discipled. If you need help with that please let us know.

And to all of you we speak this blessing:

> *The Lord bless you and keep you; the Lord make His face shine upon you, and be gracious to you; the Lord lift up His countenance upon you, and give you peace* (Numbers 6:24-26).

Chapter 18

TESTIMONIES OF HIS GRACE

But without faith it is impossible to please Him, for he who comes to God must believe that He is, and that He is a rewarder of those who diligently seek Him (Hebrews 11:6).

JOE

I am writing this bonus chapter to demonstrate the power of God in our lives. These are signs and testimonies that didn't necessarily fit in the body of this book but are important to include to help build your faith. The power of testimony cannot be underestimated in our lives. Hopefully with as many testimonies as there are in this chapter you will find one or many that resonate with you. If you do, then allow them to activate the faith the Lord has given to you to believe for the same and more.

Phone Interview

A young lady was visiting from another state where she was trying to get a job. While she was here, she got a call on her cell phone to come in for a personal interview. After she informed them that she couldn't get back in time, they told her that without being there to interview in their office in person she wouldn't be considered for the job. She came to the front of the church for prayer on this matter. Afterward, when she walked to the back of the sanctuary, she came to me and told me her story. I placed my hand on her head and while I was praying I heard the prophetic words "phone interview." Fifteen minutes later she called me on my phone and told me that the people had called her back and asked her if she could do a phone interview instead. God had changed their heart!

You Are God's Favorite

I had been telling Junior that he was God's favorite for many years. He is a wonderful brother who has a passion for the Lord and always has a smile on his face, even though his life hasn't been easy.

One Sunday Junior walked up to me and said, "Dr. Joe, you have been telling me that I'm God's favorite for a long time, but I just couldn't believe it. I'm here to tell you today that, 'I AM GOD'S FAVORITE!'" I write it like that because he wasn't just saying it with his mouth, it had finally made it to his heart and he really believed it now. His smile has gotten bigger and his passion for the Lord has gotten stronger because he now knows that he is truly loved by God. He doesn't have to do anything to earn that love. Jesus has already done everything that was needed for Junior to be infinitely loved by the Father who is Love Himself.

Make It So

I was driving to work one morning asking God to be in His Presence and I saw a license plate that read "MAKE IT SO." I believe the Lord was telling me that His Presence is always there, and if I wanted to be in it I had to just "make it so" in my own life—just live in what He has already provided.

Why Is That?

I was driving to work one day on the freeway. I was praying "Thank You, Lord, for being in Your Presence" and trying to have an attitude of "making it so" in my life. A car drove up just in front of the left side of my van with a license plate that read "Y-IS-THAT?" I pondered what it meant and spoke out loud, "Because I have stopped believing that I have to ask God for His Presence when He is already with me." God is so awesome!

God Is Good

I was in my van on the freeway driving to work and praying to see more of the power of God in my life. A car drove up on my left side and slowed down just enough ahead of me to read the license plate. It read "GODSGUD" and then it sped off. I believe the Lord was telling me that He is good and I will see His power in my life because that is His perfect will for His children.

Stop the Rain

This is really cool. It was supposed to rain on a particular day and my grass was getting very long because I was waiting for the new grass to come in after we had re-seeded. The rain clouds were thick as I started mowing. I was worshiping in song, but it began to sprinkle. I don't like to cut wet grass and I was starting to feel soggy myself. At that moment I thought about Jesus commanding the wind and the waves and they obeyed. I looked up and said, "Lord, if it's not going to affect some master atmospheric plan, I'm going to do this." I said, "In the name of Jesus, I command the rain to stop until I get done cutting this grass." It stopped! I kept worshiping. About five minutes later it started to sprinkle again. I said again, "Clouds, you need to stop raining until I get this grass cut." It stopped again and it didn't rain the rest of the day! I woke up the next morning and the ground was soaked with rain. Most people would probably think that this was coincidence. I choose to believe it was cooperation. Praise the Lord He cares about the little things too!

For the earnest expectation of the creation eagerly waits
for the revealing of the sons of God (Romans 8:19).

The Master's Key

One morning I had a dream at 5:55 a.m.. I dreamed that I was working in a hospital as an intern. I didn't see any patients, but I was interacting with the rest of the staff. I found myself in a basement room of the facility that looked like it had been dug out from a cave. The room was filled with rings of old-looking keys that I somehow knew opened individual locks to patient rooms in the hospital. Then I spotted one lone green key. All the rest were silver or brass colored. I turned to a person who had come downstairs with me and I said, "See this key? This is the Master Key." At that moment, I woke up.

I believe the interpretation of the dream is this: There are many people who are out there and are sick and hurting physically, mentally, and emotionally and need to be set free. There are many different keys that the world offers, but we have been given the Master's key. He is the giver of life (the green key), and He is offering it to us to use to free everyone we come in contact with.

Bless Them, Lord

A young man, Jason, and his wife came to me one Sunday for prayer. I asked what they wanted from the Lord. They said they were having some financial problems and wanted me to pray that God would bless them. I put my arms around both of them and prayed, "Lord, I ask that You bless them financially in every way. I pray that they will get checks in the mail, lost things found, inheritances that they didn't know they had, and people saying, 'I don't know why I'm doing this for them, but I am going to bless them.'"

That next Wednesday night I was running the video camera in the back of the church. I was praying and asking the Lord to see more of His glory, which is His character and nature being manifested on the earth. At that very moment I received a text from Jason forwarded through another man in the service. It said, "If Joe is there, if you don't mind, tell him the prayer he said over me Sunday about someone giving me extra money was answered." God had answered my prayer to see more of His glory through this brother's testimony. If we pray and bless people in the natural, the Lord will do the supernatural.

That next Sunday Jason told me the details of the story. He had done some work for a person at that man's house. When it came time for payment, the man asked him if he wanted cash or a check because if it was cash he would have to go to the bank. Jason told him that either was fine. The man gave him a check. Jason took it, folded it up, but waited until he got home to look at it. When he did open it up to look, the check was made out for more than what he had asked for. When does that ever happen? Praise God, it does when He is involved!

About a week later the Lord answered the prayer of blessing again. Jason got an unexpected raise at his job. God just continues to multiply the blessings.

I Love You

My daughter-in-law, Amanda, visited Impact Church for a special service. She was grieving over the loss of their baby through a miscarriage. I felt in my spirit that the Lord was saying to her "I love you, Amanda" and He wanted to put His arms around her. After the conclusion of the service a woman named Elena came up to her and said, "I don't know you, but I have been struggling for 20 minutes with a word for you from the Lord. God says Jesus loves you and I'm supposed to put my arms around you and hold you," which she proceeded to do. God cares about us and wants to comfort us more than we can imagine.

One Year Baby

Heidi helped Amanda move to Texas to join our son Joey who had gotten a job there. While they were in the area, they decided to visit Joan Hunter at her ministry offices. Because of Amanda's desire to have children they asked Joan to pray for her. While Joan was praying, she prophesied that Amanda would have a baby within the year. Our first grandchild, Grace, was born approximately 11 months later! The Lord will give us the desires of our heart if we trust Him. Thank You, Jesus!

Like Baby's Skin

There was a lady at church who asked us to pray for her. The skin on her face was an abnormally dark color, thick and wrinkling. She looked like she was wearing a mask. She said her doctor had diagnosed her with scleroderma, an autoimmune disease that attacks the skin and in some cases the internal organs. It is normally incurable.

We prayed over her that night and declared that she would be healed with evidence that her skin would look like baby's skin. Over the next few months the dark mask started peeling away and her skin became as soft and smooth as a baby's skin. Praise His Name!

Calf Injury Healed

Eric was playing basketball with some friends. All of a sudden he looked behind him because it felt like someone threw a fastball and hit him in the back of his lower leg. The pain was excruciating, but there was no baseball and no one had hit him.

That night he called his supervisor and told him what had happened. "I'm a runner," the supervisor said, "and from what you described to me, that's a torn calf muscle. You will be out for several weeks." The next day he went limping into work and had an awful time trying to climb the stairs to a meeting he had to attend. "What happened to you?" they asked. He told them about the injury and how it happened.

Eric called me and asked me to pray, which I did over the phone. In three days, not weeks, he was completely healed and was able to go to work with no medical intervention. He was glad that he had returned to work the day after the accident because his other supervisor said, "I can't believe that. Are you sure there was something wrong with you? That healed really fast!" But everyone else had already seen him limping in pain and knew that the injury was real. Eric just answered him, "God!" Thank You, Jesus!

Type II Diabetes Cured

A pastor friend of mine called me one day and said, "I went to the doctor today and they have diagnosed me with Type II diabetes. What should I do?" I believe that the Lord at that point pulled on my medical background and mixed it with His words of wisdom and I told her what to do. In the ensuing days her blood glucose became normal. After three months, she went back to the doctor who was surprised and said, "I have never seen this happen. You are no longer a diabetic." Not only that, but the doctor took the diagnosis out of her chart! She said that she had never done that before. When the Lord heals, He heals completely.

Not the Same Way Twice

Anita, the same lady who had the elbow healed supernaturally in Chapter 14, was having pain in the other elbow. She decided, because the pain was so severe, to have the surgery done on this elbow too. After the surgery, the doctor put her arm in a cast so that it would heal properly. This elbow started exhibiting post-operative pain similar to the one that had been healed. She asked and we prayed that this joint would be healed too. (Remember that God healed the first one supernaturally.) The Lord told her that this one wasn't going to be healed the same way, but that she was going to have to praise through it. So every week Anita would come to the front of the church and lift both arms to worship and praise the Lord.

One night during the worship service, Micole, our worship pastor, stopped singing and said that he had to tell us what God had been showing him. He said that he saw angels in the sanctuary bearing gifts and handing them out to people. He continued that these gifts were not only healing, but anything that people needed and if they would receive them, they could have them.

A few minutes later, Anita stood on the platform, tears streaming down her cheeks, and told the congregation what had just happened. Just after Micole had described the vision he had, she had felt the Lord squeeze her arm through her cast. "And you know that's impossible," she said. Immediately the pain left and hasn't come back. In fact, she had to beg her doctor to remove that cast because he was concerned her elbow wasn't healed yet.

Healing Comes in Many Forms

Like I have written before, salvation means more than just physical healing. Anita, this same person, was able to get her PhD in healthcare administration, even though she was married with several children. The problem was that after she got her degree, she couldn't find a job. She had applied for over 400 positions and no one had offered her a job. She prayed and prayed, but it seemed like God wasn't answering. She was still working as a social worker, but felt like she wasn't where she was supposed to be.

The Lord showed her that she was having a tremendous impact for the Kingdom right where she was. In fact, she had prayed for someone who had clinically died from a heart attack and they came back to life. Once she understood the importance of being obedient to stay where the Lord had placed her for the greater good, she said, "Lord, if I never become an administrator and You want me to stay a social worker, that's okay with me." Within a week she was offered a job to be an administrator-in-training working for an administrator whom she had worked for before. She said that if she had her pick of a job that would have been it. As of this writing, she will be a full-fledged administrator before the end of the year.

I wish I had room here to tell you all the miracles Anita has told us about, but it would fill another book. She understands the true meaning of God's grace and that she is His favorite.

He Who Has Ears, Let Him Hear

I went to an Eastside Church men's retreat one weekend. There were over 50 men in attendance and most of them came back changed with a greater understanding of their value and identity in the Kingdom. One man I met, named Rich, told me that he had burst his left eardrum in a scuba-diving accident years before. The eardrum had never healed back together again and he had very little hearing and constant pain and buzzing in that ear, especially when things got quiet.

One night at the retreat, while we were in the hayloft of an old barn with a tin roof, we were praying over each other that God would place His mantle upon each one of us. I asked Rich if I could pray for his ear. As I prayed the sky seemed like it broke open and the rain came down in torrents. The sound was so loud on the tin roof that we could hardly hear anything else. As soon as we were done praying, it stopped, followed by quiet. Rich looked at me and said, "I'm speechless," which is very unusual for Rich, and he stayed that way for a long time.

Later I found out that not only were the pain and buzzing in his ear gone, but that God had also done a deep work in his life. An issue that had happened when he was in the military, which he hadn't forgiven himself for, was healed instantly in his heart. He was free and his face showed it. Tears flowed from his eyes. "I don't normally cry," he said. "You have seen more tears today than my wife has ever seen." To him this was even a greater miracle than the healing of his ear.

Later on that night, Rich also told us about lower back problems that he had been suffering with. He said that when it rains he has numbness and pain in his legs and his muscles get so weak he can hardly walk. Brannon, our care pastor, and I prayed for him. The next day it was raining heavily. When I asked how he was doing, he said his legs were doing great. "Normally," he said, "my legs would be so bad I would have trouble walking if it was raining like this."

Two months later, Rich excitedly approached me after one of the church services. He was sitting beside his wife during praise and worship and he actually started to hear her with the ear that had been healed from the pain and buzzing. During the next two months his hearing got better and better. He decided to make an appointment with the doctor he has been going to for many years, who is familiar with his injury, and have it checked out. When Rich told him the testimony of how he was healed, the doctor was skeptical until he looked into his ear canal. God had done a restorative miracle. The doctor found that the eardrum, which had been ruptured for almost 28 years, had completely grown back together and there was just minimal scar tissue left. He was amazed. Rich says, "I think I can hear out of that ear better than the other one!" Thank You, Jesus!

Dyslexia Is No Match for Jesus

Richard, a friend of ours, felt the call of God on his life to become a preacher. He wanted to be ordained under Joan Hunter Ministries just as we were. But in order to do that there was quite a number of books that had to be read and studied, as well as many hours of video teaching. The problem was that Richard had dyslexia and reading was extremely difficult for him, as anyone with dyslexia can tell you. Reading all those books before the next ordination school would have been impossible for him in the natural. He asked us to pray that he would be able to read the books so he could become ordained.

The Lord answered his request. "It's like being an un-caged animal," he said. "I read so fast my eyes would cross." He could read for hours on end and comprehend what he was reading. When he got done with one book, he just felt compelled to pick up the next one and keep reading. He said he could never do that before. In the next several months he not only read all the books but had fulfilled all the other prerequisites too.

While he was at ordination school, the students all lined up to be prayed for. When Joan laid her hands on him, she prophesied over him. "You have been made fun of because of your short height," she proclaimed, "but not anymore. You are a David who is going to slay many giants." As soon as she said those words the power of God went through him like electricity and he hit the ground shaking. "I have never felt anything like that!" he exclaimed. That experience has given him confidence like he has never had before.

Right now as I'm writing this, with great appreciation for livestreaming, I'm watching Richard walking across the stage to receive his Certificate of Ordination. Our God is Lord over every name including dyslexia! When He calls us, He will make a way.

He Is Still Speaking

I was praying this morning on my way to work and thinking about the section in Chapter 8 where we talk about why we don't see everyone we pray for healed. I was asking the Lord to be able to hear Him more clearly for more miracles and healings, not because it makes us look good but because it shows others His goodness and that He still does miracles and that awakens people to Him.

I started singing, without thinking, "You Make Me Brave" by Amanda Cook. But I was singing, "You call me out beyond the storm into the waves." I thought, "That's not how that goes. It is 'out beyond the shore into the waves.'" Just then the traffic slowed down to a crawl. There was a large truck hauling lumber three vehicles ahead of me. Now we were crawling about ten miles an hour. I looked down at the license plate on the car directly in front of me and it read "OFFSHOR1."

I immediately made the connection between the song, the incident with Peter and Jesus walking on the water, and what I had prayed. In my mind I heard the Holy Spirit say, "You are, and need to be more of, an 'off shore one.' One who will ask Me, like Peter, to do the supernatural things I'm doing even if others aren't stepping out and doing them. That's where the miraculous happens." And like Peter, I need to do this even if I only get part of it right. Better to take a few steps into the miraculous than none at all. Jesus is still there to help us and let us know where we went wrong so we can do better the next time.

I believe the Lord allowed the traffic to back up so I would pay attention and also so I could take a picture and video of the car. He does things like that. I have included the picture so you can see it for yourself.

I looked up the song when I got to work and found it also says, *"So I will let You draw me out beyond the shore into Your grace."* The definition of grace I like best is this: "The supernatural Presence of God, who empowers us to be able to do more than we can do on our own, the very works of God, and become who we were created to be."

> *So then faith cometh by hearing, and hearing by the word of God* (Romans 10:17 KJV).

FINAL WORDS

This book is a faithful representation of what has actually happened in our lives and the lives of those cited in its pages. The words and principles have been reviewed and affirmed by those we trust as understanding and rightly dividing the Word of God. We have followed up on every testimony we were able to and had each person validate their story's accuracy.

Heidi and I hope this book has challenged you. God is always speaking. Will you listen? He wants to manifest His glory on the earth. Will you let Him do that through you? He wants to do things beyond your imagination. Will you do the natural so He can do the supernatural? He is looking for children who will re-present Him well. Will you become one of those sons or daughters that look just like Jesus?

If you answered yes to those questions, then this last verse is for you.

> *For the eyes of the Lord run to and fro throughout the whole earth, to show Himself strong on behalf of those whose heart is loyal to Him* (2 Chronicles 16:9).

ABOUT THE AUTHORS

Dr. Joe Wadlinger and his wife, Heidi, have a burning passion to bring total wholeness of body, soul, spirit and provision to the world through the true Gospel of the Lord Jesus Christ. They are both ordained ministers under Joan Hunter Ministries in Tomball, Texas, and attend Eastside Church in Charlotte, North Carolina. The Lord has given them a mission to encourage people to embrace their God-given destinies and let them know the incredible love the Father has for every one of us. As they love to declare, "We are all God's favorites."

They live in Charlotte, North Carolina, along with their three sons, Joey, Jonathan, and Joshua as well as Joey's wife, Amanda, and their four daughters.

For more information, encouraging teaching and resources, please go to their website at www.EncouragingPeople.com.

Experience a personal revival!

Spirit-empowered content from today's top Christian authors delivered directly to your inbox.

Join today!
lovetoreadclub.com

Inspiring Articles
Powerful Video Teaching
Resources for Revival

Get all of this and so much more, e-mailed to you twice weekly!

LOVE TO READ CLUB
by **D DESTINY IMAGE**

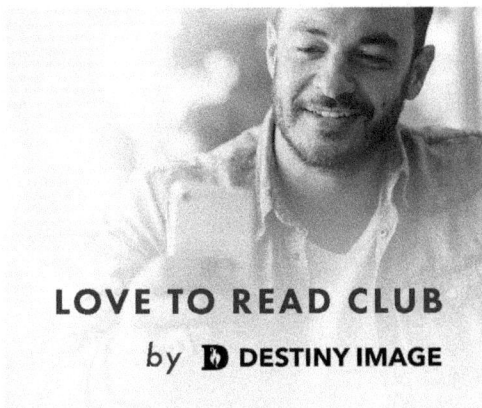

www.ingramcontent.com/pod-product-compliance
Lightning Source LLC
Chambersburg PA
CBHW070824100426
42813CB00003B/481